And THAT
Started A FIGHT . . .

TODAY IS OK. TOMORROW HAS PROMISE.
THE PAST HAS SOME GREAT
STORIES AND TIMES.

Doug

And THAT
Started A FIGHT . . .

Growing Up before
Dodgeball Was Illegal

Doug Brooks and Tom Wikiera

MOUNTAIN ARBOR
PRESS

MOUNTAIN ARBOR
PRESS
Alpharetta, GA

The authors have tried to recreate events, locations, and conversations from their memories of them. They have made every effort to give credit to the source of any images, quotes, or other material contained within and obtain permissions when feasible.

ISBN: 978-1-63183-951-1

Printed in the United States of America   0 2 0 8 2 1

⊗This paper meets the requirements of ANSI/NISO Z39.48-1992 (Permanence of Paper)

Photo credits: Shelly Croyle and Jody A. Boucher of the *Woonsocket Call*

Illustrations by Professor Mark Stephen Smith

This book is dedicated to John Wikiera and Kevin Lynch, two great friends who left us far too soon.

Contents

Introduction   *ix*

The Early Sixties   1
The Gift of Sharing   11
The Toilet Bowl   15
The Post Office   23
Pack of Lies   29
Robby Rabbit   37
Poison Sumac   41
Banana Ball   45
Carrying the Worms   53
Recognition   57
The Three-Dollar Lure   61
Hook to the Head   65
Impulse   69
Driving without a License   73
Glad the Horse   77
The Trip to Fenway Park   83
Park League Sports   89
Par for the Course   97
Shooting the Rapids   105
The End   111

Acknowledgments   *115*

Introduction

Remember your pals from when you were twelve or thirteen years old? The guys you hung with every day. Whether it was in school, at the ballpark, or just hanging out, these were your best friends. I remember those days and want to share some of my exploits and adventures. It is my sincere hope that, as you read this book, recollections from your childhood will come flooding back. Memories, names, and faces you haven't thought of or heard for many years will rise to the surface and make you smile.

At my age, my contact with kids is limited, so I rely on my friends telling me about their grandkids. Though some of their stories are funny, from what I hear these poor kids have little or no free time. Every minute of every day is scheduled, supervised, and accounted for, whether it's school, practice, or mind-numbing screen time. I think if you took a group of these kids (without their cell phones or tablets), put them on a field, gave them a ball, and told them to make up some games and have fun, many would be lost. And the one who stood up and took charge would be considered a bully, banned from the group, and sent to counseling. Without an adult to organize them, they would probably moan and groan about having nothing to do and demand the return of their electronic devices.

We grew up as children of the Greatest Generation; our fathers were WWII veterans. They survived the Great Depression of the 1930s and then a world war. After the war, they returned home, got married, and raised us, the

Baby Boomer generation. Our fathers weren't our friends. They didn't refer to us as their pals or buddies. When told to clean our bedrooms, we didn't hear, "Hey buddy, can you do me a favor and clean your room?" Or "The trash needs to go out. Can you take care of that for me, pal?" No, we were expected to do what we were told when we were told to do it, no negotiations. We were loved, but we were not decision makers.

Compared to today, we grew up in the technological dark ages. It was a time with limited technology—AM radio and TV with three channels. Our entertainment was our responsibility, with sports as our outlet. We played games according to the season, where we were, and how many guys were there to play. We played dodgeball before it was outlawed and became a felonious activity. Tackle football was not out of the question. Read the "Banana Ball" chapter to see what a stingray could do. We were active, we had fun, and we were not fat. Some of our endeavors may have been questionable, and without a doubt somewhat dangerous, but we enjoyed them and lived to tell the tales.

After high school, I left Woonsocket, Rhode Island, to attend the University of Tampa. I returned to Woonsocket during school breaks but remained in Tampa after graduation. I made occasional trips north to visit my dad and friends, but as the years passed, my visits became less frequent.

It was sometime around 1995 and I was on a work assignment in Boston. I called my old friend Tom Wikiera to see if we could get together for a beer. It had been a few years since we had last seen each other. He enhanced my visit by calling his brother John, Kevin Lynch, and Jimmy O'Brien (Obie), the cast of characters from our early years.

We got together at a popular sports bar in Woonsocket. It had been many years since the five of us were together and it was a fun evening. We spent hours recalling the ball games and crazy things we did as kids, wondering how we survived. And as usual, there were arguments about who did what to whom. John, in his soft, professorial tone, would say, "Tom, I think you're mistaken." Tom would fire back, "You're nuts. I know exactly what happened." Kevin and I would laugh, then Obie would say, "You're both wrong." And it would go around again. The topic didn't matter; this was the format. It was a great night. We drank a few beers and laughed a lot, but unfortunately, the evening had to end. That was the last time the five us were together.

About a year after that evening, I started writing about our adventures, not with the intention of publishing a book, but as a reminder of the fun things we did as kids. A few years later, I was back in Boston and told Tom about my writings. We started talking and the stories started to flow. Over the years, Tom, in Massachusetts, and I, in Florida/Georgia, told these stories to our friends and got two reactions: laughter and wonder that we stayed out of the hospital emergency room. Tom and I were best friends and teammates as kids. He remained in the Woonsocket area and maintained contact with many of our childhood friends, who provided reminders and details of our escapades, so it was only natural that I enlist him as my writing partner. *And THAT Started A FIGHTt . . .* was in motion.

Read and enjoy our stories. Tom, John, Kevin, Obie, and I had a great time living these escapades. Tom and I had a lot of fun writing them.

The Early Sixties

"I know you, I know you, and I know you."

"Yeah, then who am I?" asked John with his typical smartass attitude.

"Never mind who you are, but I know who you are," she answered.

Old Lady Coreleone had a big backyard with the best fruit trees around—apple, pear, peach, and plum trees laden with fresh, delicious fruit just waiting to be picked. And who better to pick said fruit than five hungry boys? She also had a mean dog, a meaner son, and a chain-link fence to protect her fruit and keep us out. She had resources; we liked fruit. Guess who won?

And THAT Started A FIGHT . . .: Growing Up before Dodgeball Was Illegal is a collection of short stories recounting the episodes of five friends, Tom, John, Kevin, Jim (Obie), and myself during the early sixties in the New England city of Woonsocket, Rhode Island.

Tom and John were brothers who were vastly different people, and though they didn't really like each other, they spent every day together, which generated a lot of animosity. Their fights weren't knockdown punches to the face but mainly shots to the arm or slaps to the back of the head, often followed by a crippling charley horse to the thigh. There were also wrestling matches that ended with Tom on top and John crying for Tom to get off. Inevitably, Tom would let him get up and John would give him a shove to restart the fight. Their fights were similar to the early days of boxing, when rounds weren't timed but ended when one of the fighters was knocked down and the bout was over when one of the contestants couldn't answer the bell. And if the Wikiera boys did not have a reason to fight, there was always Obie the instigator to generate controversy.

Ninety percent of the fights were between Tom and John, and the remaining 10 percent were usually just disagreements among the rest of us. The antagonism between Tom and John began many years earlier, probably about the time they learned to walk and talk. Like the feud between the Hatfields and McCoys, the Wikiera strife lasted for decades. They loved each other as brothers and would always stand up for each other against anyone else, but one on one, they were enemies. You will read about the beginning of their feud in "The Gift of Sharing."

Many of our stories take place during the summer, but stories like "The Toilet Bowl," "The Post Office," and "Shooting the Rapids" took place during the winter months. Bad weather rarely got in the way of our getting outside to play some sort of game. And not every story has a fight; some are just amusing.

As you read our tales, you will see that our goal is to entertain and relate what it was like to be a kid in the good old days before political correctness, playdates, and video games. Most of our free time was spent outside, playing whatever sport was in season. If we couldn't play outside, we went to the YMCA to participate in whatever sport was offered that day. It didn't matter whether it was basketball, volleyball, or gymnastics; we were there to participate. Some of our games got intense. We were best friends, but that didn't stop us from arguing, calling each other names, and generating hard fouls. Wimps we were not.

Any hard feelings usually passed when the game ended, or at least by the next day. Time moved on and the years rolled by, and so did we, but we remained lifelong friends.

John was the youngest of the group. He was good-looking with a thin, medium build and silky blonde hair, unassuming and pleasant. He was a fast runner with quick moves that made him a talented athlete. Those gifts were accompanied by sneaky and devious thought processes, which often led his cohorts and him into bad situations.

Tom, John's brother and twenty months older, was the senior of the group. Where John was thin, Tom was stocky, but also an exceptionally talented athlete. He was quick, and when he needed to be, just as fast as John. Tom was strong, which, combined with his speed, made him a formidable opponent in any sport. Years later, Tom showed that power as a high school fullback and later as a college linebacker. He was a left-handed pitcher, and, of all the pitchers around Woonsocket, one of the best. John was quiet and sneaky; Tom was loud and straightforward.

Kevin was similar to John—smart, athletic, and born with the wittiness common to those of Irish heritage. Those similarities, and the penchant for sneakiness, drew John and him together, especially when the group had to vote on something. Kevin differed from the rest of us in that he was just flat-out lazy. He would often sleep until noon, and when he wasn't sleeping, he was almost always looking for the easy way out. He also had a forehead so large that we always wanted to see if we could watch movies on it.

Obie was an enigma. He was tall and thin and NOT the sharpest tool in the shed. But he did show some cleverness. One day, he got in trouble in school for talking during class. The teacher told him to write an essay on "Silence Is Golden." He wrote it, and it began, "Silence is

3

golden because someone must have painted it. He must have done a good job because lots of people talk about it." Assignment completed. Not exactly what the teacher was expecting, but Obie completed the task. No one ever knew what he was going to say or do, and he really didn't care. He was an exceptional baseball player and a good all-around athlete. He didn't invent "trash talk," but he was an early devotee. He thoroughly enjoyed the conflicts he caused inside and outside of our group. He was the wildest and often proved to be the tiebreaker in many of our disputes, usually siding with John and Kevin. He didn't share their prowess at sneakiness; he never even considered holding back. His ready, fire, aim process led to many good plans going foul.

Doug was the quiet one, more thoughtful before speaking or acting than the others. In retrospect, he may have been the voice of reason that no one at this age was even going to consider. He was smart and a worker who didn't have all the God-given athletic abilities of the others, but more than made up for it with effort and desire. His tenacity paid off. In high school, he won the student athlete scholarship award. He was built like Tom, strong and rugged. Because of their similarities they tended to side together and set the stage for many of the future conflicts.

Summer in Woonsocket was a wonderful time for boys with energy, imagination, and time on their hands. We were free-range kids decades before the term was coined and later became a form of child abuse. On summer days, we left our homes in the morning and often didn't return until suppertime. We rode our bikes on the streets *without* adult supervision or helmets. Holy crap! By today's standards, our parents would have been in jail.

We were young, so world events really didn't mean a

lot to us; but we were good students. We glanced at the headlines in the *Woonsocket Call*, our local newspaper. John F. Kennedy was president and wildly popular with Woonsocket's Catholic population—be they French, Italian, or Irish; John Glenn magically orbited the earth three times; and Johnny Carson took over *The Tonight Show* (as if we were allowed to stay up that late). "Snail mail" was all people used, and for four cents a letter, sent first-class, could cross the country in about a week.

We more than glanced at the sports pages. We were heavily into sports and considered ourselves athletes. Actually, we thought we were great athletes. We followed professional baseball, football, and basketball. In New England, everyone was either a Boston Red Sox or New York Yankee fan. We were Sox fans. Except for New Year's Day bowl games, we didn't pay much attention to college sports, but we were big fans of Providence College basketball. PC had a great center, six-foot-ten John Thompson, who, after college, played for the Celtics and later coached Georgetown, winning the NCAA championship in 1984. PC also had a guard named Vinnie Ernst, who was five foot eight, a size we could relate to.

The early sixties' Boston Red Sox seasons were typical for that era. They usually finished somewhere in the middle of the pack or worse in the American League. Losing to the Yankees was a common theme that continued for many years. But as bad as they were as a team, we loved the Sox and their great players. Dick Radatz and Bill Monbouquette were fantastic pitchers on a bad team. Pitcher Gene Conley was a fantastic two-sport athlete who also played in the NBA. The Sox had future Hall of Famer Carl Yastrzemski playing left field, who, in the 1967 season, would win the Triple Crown. Tony Conigliaro, a local kid from Revere, Massachusetts, hit a home run in his first at bat at Fenway Park.

In the fall, we were fans of the New York Giants in the NFL and the Boston Patriots in the AFL. The Giants went 12-2 in 1962 but lost to the Green Bay Packers in the NFL championship game. They had a great team with Y. A. Tittle as their quarterback, Sam Huff at middle linebacker, and All-Pro Frank Gifford at running back. Many sports fans will remember Frank Gifford more for his many years of Emmy Award–winning game coverage on *Monday Night Football* with Howard Cosell than for his twelve-year playing career.

The Boston Patriots fielded their first team in 1960, and because Boston was close to Woonsocket, we became Patriots fans. Their first couple of years were rocky, but they had a solid team in 1962 with nine wins, four losses, and a tie to finish in second place. Their most memorable players were Babe Parilli at quarterback, Gino Cappelletti as kicker and split end (back then, some players played multiple positions), and Nick Buoniconti playing middle linebacker.

The Celtics, perennial champions, beat the Lakers for the 1962 NBA championship. The Celtics and Lakers were fierce rivals many years before the Larry Bird and Magic Johnson era came along.

A BRIEF HISTORY
OF WOONSOCKET

Woonsocket Falls Village was founded in the 1820s and its fortunes expanded as the Industrial Revolution took root. With the Blackstone River flowing through the city providing ample waterpower, the region became a prime location for textile mills.

Woonsocket as an official town was not established until 1867, when three villages, Woonsocket Falls, Social, and Jenckesville, officially became the town of Woonsocket. In 1871, four additional industrial villages, Smithfield, Hamlet, Bernon, and Globe, were added to the town, establishing its present boundaries. Woonsocket was incorporated as a city in 1888. I mention the villages because as time marched on, even though Woonsocket was a city, each section of the city retained some of its village's identity.

Large numbers of French Canadians emigrated to Woonsocket to work in the textile mills. I couldn't say if they were documented or undocumented; it wasn't a political issue back then. And with them came French-language newspapers, radio programs, and even some movies. Most conversations in public were in French or a combination of French/English that generated some very funny phrases that still exist today. Here are a few of the Woonsocketeze phrases:

> Woonsocket was a place where people "parked their cars side by each."
> "Went 'unting (hunting) wit dere twice-barrel shotgun."
> "Got ground in their look" (dirt in their eyes).
> "Tro me down the stairs my at" (throw me my hat).
> "There it was. Gone!"

When rambunctious kids would use French Canadians' property as a shortcut you could hear the owners scream, "Next time you cut through my yard, go 'round!"

During our formative years, Woonsocket was a mill town, primarily textile, with a few other industries mixed in. Woonsocket High School had a high dropout rate. Many kids quit school at age sixteen to follow in their parents' footsteps and work in the mills. Recent headlines have parents being sent to jail for bribing college officials to admit their kids. That wouldn't have happened in Woonsocket. Regrettably, a lot of the mill-working parents believed that if the mills were good enough for them, they were good enough for their kids. Fortunately, our parents didn't have that mindset and neither did we. We didn't spend much time discussing our futures, but the one thing we agreed on and were 100 percent sure of was that we would not be mill rats.

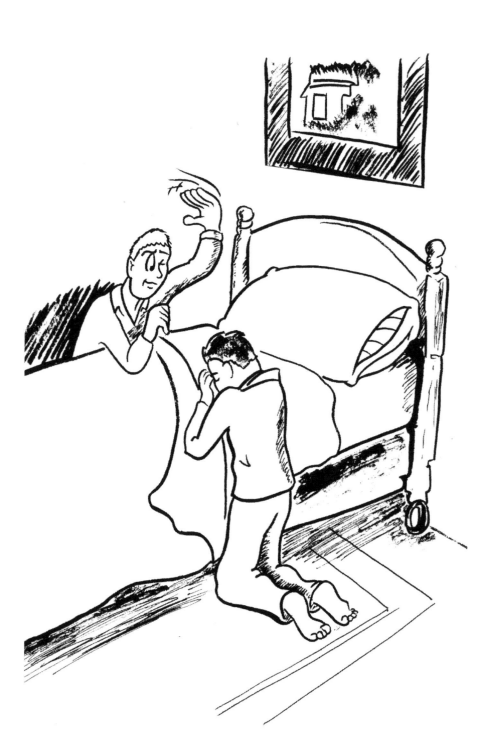

The Gift of Sharing

Share and share alike, that's what all of us are taught. Sharing is integral to growing up with siblings, especially when they are close in age, since the closer they are in age, the more they are forced to share. Slightly worn but still-good T-shirts, perfectly fine pants that are a few inches too short with a patch or two, and a bike with just a bit of rust and some missing spokes are just some of the things eventually, and resentfully, shared; not to mention routine daily chores, special privileges, and physical space. Though parents never seem to grasp the concept, anecdotal evidence suggests that the more that children are forced to share, the less likely they willingly do so. Such was the case with Tom and John.

When they were young, Tom and John lived with their parents and their maternal grandfather. They shared just about everything and hated every minute of it. Interestingly, the one thing that caused the most animosity and battles among them was sharing a bed. Unlike today's need for every child to rightfully have his privacy preserved, in middle-class fifties and sixties it was common for young siblings to sleep together due to lack of housing space. As a prudent necessity, sharing a bed resulted in becoming the initial battleground for the Wikiera brothers' lifetime of disputes.

Conflict began each evening, ironically, at prayer time. Prior to retiring for the night, they would kneel and say their prayers. Before "amen," they would pass out the blessings. John would usually start with something like, "Bless Mom, Dad, Grandma, Grandpa, me, and Jerkface." Responses generally included "Dope, Idiot, Retard, Dirtbag," and then proceeded to get downright nasty. Kneeling across the bed from each other made it easy to find a target and land a punch.

The real fun started when they climbed into their standard double bed. In the summer, it was usually so hot and sticky that neither one wanted to be near the other, so fights for territory were short-lived. Cooler weather caused things to paradoxically heat up. Tom thought that thirty inches across belonged to him, and twenty-six to John. John felt that Tom had the math reversed.

"You're on my side of the bed," Tom would start. "Push over."

"No, I'm not!" John would reply. "You're on my side— move!"

Then, like two sumo wrestlers, they would jockey for position. Back to back, they'd push and shove while the mandatory name-calling escalated. All of this had to be done quietly so that their father wouldn't hear them. The fear of waking him—especially on a work night—and its repercussions was the one thing the battling duo could agree on.

The headboard and footboard of their battlefield each had an indentation directly in the middle, which served as the perfect territorial divider. The boys would take turns drawing lines from the top to the bottom, splitting the bed evenly and claiming their portions. The tough part about being back to back was that neither participant could see if he was winning or losing ground. Eventually, they had to face each other. Lying there face to face and inches apart meant it was easier to push, slap, and punch each other, which could only lead to one end. A fight broke out. By then, everyone in the three-family apartment building could hear what was going on. Inevitably, in walked their father reaching for his belt. They both knew what that would mean—a whack on the ass, yet another experience they hated to share. Curiously, even though supposedly family classics, David and Ricky Nelson never experienced such from Ozzie; and Ward Cleaver never pulled a belt on Wally and the Beav. And, surely, in a few short years in future television, "Goodnights" at the Walton house bore absolutely no resemblance to Tom and John's nightly ritual. Apparently, art does *not* imitate reality—at least not the reality at the Wikiera place. A few years later, the family moved to a larger apartment and each brother had his own room, but the seeds of discontent had been sown and there were many more battles on the horizon.

The Toilet Bowl

Summer was transitioning to fall. The leaves were changing from green to orange to red and the weather was getting cooler. And it was football season.

This particular fall brought us something new and exciting: tackle football. Not pickup games in the park, but organized football with uniforms, pads, and coaches. Pop Warner Football was coming to Woonsocket and the Italian Workingmen's Club (IWC) was going to sponsor a team. Kevin, Obie, Tom, and John decided to try out for the team. I can't remember why I missed the tryouts (I may have been pumping gas at the Flying A gas station) and didn't play that season, but I did attend games to support my friends.

We played a lot of tackle football games at Cold Spring Park, but this would be different. The idea of real games with rules and referees played on regulation fields with scoreboards and clocks excited everyone. Games would be played against teams from Massachusetts and Rhode Island. We were going big time!

The league came with restrictions; players had to be between ten and twelve years old. The weight range was a minimum seventy pounds and could not exceed one hundred. Therein lay the only potential problem: the weight limit. Tom, Obie, and Kevin fit perfectly, but John was just over sixty pounds, sixty-five after a big meal and fully dressed in his winter clothing. Fortunately, we considered ourselves expert problem solvers, so a few pounds were not going to give us trouble. John was thin and a picky eater with a fast metabolism. While his mother forced him to clean his plate at every meal, we knew that he still wasn't going to make weight. Kevin said, "If he needs more weight, we'll just have to give it to him." Tom and I looked at each other and realized where he was headed. As self-respecting fishermen, each of us had a variety of lead sinkers in our tackle boxes. On Friday afternoon, we weighed John on the Y's scales to determine how many lead weights he needed to make weight and how he could hide them in his pockets. Everything looked good. And so it was that on "weigh-in Saturday," John tipped the scales at exactly seventy pounds!

We considered ourselves athletes—quick, somewhat smart (not like Fredo in *The Godfather II*), in good shape, and coachable. The guys went to the tryouts, worked hard, and made the team. Getting selected wasn't easy, considering the competition consisted of kids from all over Woonsocket plus the sons of IWC members. Tom was a running back, linebacker, and co-captain; Kevin and John were quarterbacks and safeties (defensive backs); and Obie was an end (receiver). At ninety-eight pounds, Tom was the biggest guy on the team.

The first season could not have started out better. With cheerleaders (sisters of players and daughters of IWC members) and parents in the stands cheering, the first game was a 19-0 thrashing of the Cumberland Colts, our rivals from the town next door. Unfortunately, the next game didn't go as well as expected and we lost 26-14 to the Seekonk Tigers from nearby Massachusetts. No one likes losing and the IWC coaches liked it even less. You may find this hard to believe, but back then, coaches yelled at players, and to drive home a message, they gave players an occasional slap to the back of the helmet (child abuse, call the cops). That defeat proved to be the last loss of the season. The team channeled the coaches' yelling and head slaps into wins. The next game was a win against the defending champions, Darlington, followed by six more wins, setting IWC up for the championship game against the East Providence Mohawks. Kevin was a real standout in that game, running the offense and scoring on a thirty-six-yard quarterback keeper. He also intercepted a pass at a crucial time to stop an East Providence drive. The guys had indeed made the big time. IWC in its first season won the league championship! More importantly, IWC made every player on the team an honorary Italian.

That season was memorable for two additional reasons, one being weekly Italian meals. Woonsocket had a large Italian population with multiple Italian clubs around the city, but the IWC was the largest. Downstairs was the bar, pinball machines, and pool table. Above that was the banquet hall and kitchen. After every game, the team and I went to the IWC tired and hungry. We played pinball and pool as we waited for our proud fathers to finish celebrating the games' victories in the bar. It seemed that almost every weekend there was a wedding, baby shower, or anniversary taking place in IWC's banquet hall. One Sunday, one of the cooks came into the bar to find out if we had won. The team gave her a rundown of the game (more than she wanted to hear), each player emphasizing his starring role. She listened and asked a few football questions, followed by the important one: "Are you guys hungry?" There just happened to be some leftovers upstairs and she marched us up the back stairs to the kitchen and fed us a fantastic Italian meal of spaghetti and meatballs and loaves of warm, buttery garlic bread. This became a highly anticipated weekly post-game bonus.

The other especially memorable event was the championship banquet. Over three hundred people crowded the banquet hall at the IWC to honor us. Among those speaking was Clem Labine, a Rhode Island native from nearby Lincoln, who pitched for the Brooklyn and Los Angeles Dodgers. The other speaker was one of our heroes, Andy Robustelli, a defensive end for the New York Giants. During the early days of professional sports, players didn't have multimillion-dollar contracts and endorsements, so they had to speak at banquets like ours to generate some income in the off-season. We were in disbelief and awe to have real-life pro athletes attend our event.

The championship high lasted until January 1. It was New Year's Day, the traditional final day of the college football season. Football was in our blood and we were ready to watch the bowl games on our only TV channels, ABC, NBC, and CBS. Because the fall was spent practicing and playing, we rarely watched any regular season games. We got ready to binge-watch (today's term) the season-ending Orange Bowl (Nebraska vs. Auburn), Sugar Bowl (Alabama vs. Mississippi), Cotton Bowl (Texas vs. Navy), and the granddaddy of all of them, the Rose Bowl (Illinois vs. Washington). Kevin, Tom, John, and I settled in at noon to watch the Cotton Bowl featuring Texas, who won this game to become the consensus national champs, and Navy with Heisman Trophy–winning quarterback Roger Staubach. We watched the kickoff and a couple sets of downs before John said, "Let's have our own bowl game." We didn't need much convincing. It was a cold, wet, raw day, but why would we want to watch football inside when we could be playing outside?

I had an epiphany. "We'll call it the Toilet Bowl!" I screamed. I was positive that no one had ever used "Toilet Bowl" to describe a football game.

Walking in the middle of the streets to avoid the puddles of slush, we made the short trek to Cold Spring Park. The front part of the park along Harris Avenue has a good-sized open rectangular area, about fifty yards long by twenty yards wide surrounded by trees. On a recent trip to Woonsocket, I went to Cold Spring Park and walked off the dimensions just to see if memory served me correctly—or exaggerated, as memory is apt to do—and the field actually was about fifty yards by twenty yards. Unlike the Pop Warner fields, this one didn't have green grass with white chalk lines. We weren't surrounded by thousands of rabid, screaming fans like the bowl games on TV. What we did have was a grassy area in a public park that became the site of our inaugural New Year's Day Toilet Bowl game.

Two large oak trees at each end of the field marked the goal lines. One sideline was a hill and the other side was lined with oak and elm trees. Making teams was easy. It always was. Tom and John had to be on opposing teams. Kevin always sided with John, and I with Tom. Power versus speed in Tom's and my minds. In Kevin's and John's minds, it was their superior intellect against our caveman brawn. We unanimously decided that playing tackle was the only way that this could be a legitimate bowl game.

We played a lot of pickup tackle football, but the tackles we employed weren't the "stick your face in the runner's belly, wrap your arms around him, and drive him to the ground" type of tackle taught by the IWC coaches. We didn't dive for knees, rather grabbed the runner around the waist or high on the shoulders and either rode or threw him to the ground rugby style.

Our rules were quite simple. The kickoff wasn't a kick

but a high throw down the field. One player would catch it and his teammate would sometimes block. Offensively, this was strictly a passing game. One player would hike the ball to the other then go out for a pass. There were no first downs; either the team scored in four downs or punted, which, like the kickoff, was a high throw down the field. The defense had a rusher who had to wait three seconds before he could rush, and a deep back.

John and Kevin received the initial kickoff and weaved their way down the field for a touchdown. Tom and I didn't have their finesse, so on the ensuing kickoff, I caught the ball, lateraled to Tom, and he took off down the field. Kevin jumped on his back to bring him down. That didn't work. Tom merely dragged Kevin down the field and scored to tie the game.

Friendship had no place in this game; we all wanted to win. The action was fast, the hitting and tackling were hard. When trees are used as goal lines and there are no chalk lines, the exact goal line is inevitably questioned. Tom and I tackled John somewhere close to what could be considered the goal line as Kevin threw up his hands and screamed, "Touchdown!" We weren't convinced. To prove that John wasn't in the end zone we had to look from one tree to the other. John and Kevin were known to be devious cheaters. Both of us knew that John and Kevin would move the ball as soon as we got up. Tom found an easy remedy. As he was getting up from the tackle, he put his hand on the back of John's head and shoved it into the mud while I looked down the line. "Now we know exactly where the ball is," he proclaimed—resulting in the first round of a fight destined to "go the distance." There were no penalties, just arguments about what *should* have been a penalty. We each had our illegal specialties; John was a biter, Kevin threw dirt or mud, and Tom would step on hands not picked up quickly. I sometimes used a claw-like pinch.

Halftime ended with Kevin and John up 35 to 28. We walked up to Pop's, the corner store, and being ignorant of our vital need for electrolytes and constant hydration, opted for some coffee milk. Never had coffee milk? Try it if you are ever in the Woonsocket area.

The fast-paced scoring of the first half slowed down. Back and forth we went. The game was long, but for the sake of keeping your interest, I will not describe every play. Tom and I tied the game at 35 to 35. It didn't matter the sport; John and Kevin against Tom and me were well matched. By now, we were tired, cold, and muddy, but not bloody. Not yet! We decided that the next touchdown would win. John and Kevin were driving down the field and close to a score when I boxed John in and he threw a jump pass to Kevin, who made a great catch just short of the goal line. He tried to make a move on Tom, who wasn't fooled and grabbed Kevin up high in what I thought was an effort to bring him down. Instead, he spun Kevin around and threw him back first into the tree serving as goal post. As John went to help the scratched, bruised, and now bloodied Kevin, Tom yelled, "You win!" John shoved Tom and, yep, that started a fight.

The Post Office

One winter evening an exceptionally fierce storm dropped about ten inches of snow on Woonsocket. Before Weather.com, cell phone weather apps, and overly precautious notifications from schools fearful of litigation, we simply listened to our local radio station, WWON, hoping to hear that school would be cancelled due to the hazardous conditions. But that morning, we waited in vain. Woonsocket schools would be open. In today's protective, cautious environment, schools would have closed under the threat of a storm since, due to "global warming," it could be the worst storm ever and precious, overindulged, and overweight children may have to actually touch the white stuff or get their feet wet getting to and from their parents' hybrids and SUVs. But I digress. We burned up the phone lines calling each other to formulate our plans for the day. After much deliberation, we decided that, considering the conditions, it certainly would be too dangerous to go to school. A nice, gentle rain had come down on top of the snow creating a thin layer of crunchy ice, making it far too precarious, so we reasoned, for walking to school. However, such conditions also created a perfect surface for extremely fast sliding on sheets of cardboard.

So, on a frigid January morning, we set out. We decided that we needed the biggest hill we could find to maximize our sliding thrills. The best hill was the one next to the path to Cold Spring Park. Our sliding chute would be over a hundred feet long with a very steep angle that we estimated to be about forty-five degrees. There was one potential problem—the hill ended at the Blackstone River. The Blackstone River was very pretty as it meandered its way through the city of Woonsocket, but for all intents and purposes, it was dead. There were no fish, no frogs, no turtles, absolutely nothing alive in the Woonsocket section of the river. You certainly could not swim in it. Over the many decades, the waste products dumped from the textile mills that sustained much of Woonsocket's population killed every living creature in the river. We witnessed the dyes from the mills flow into the river; blue dye one day, red the next. My guess is that when the mills started dumping their polluted dyes into the Blackstone, no one knew that the pollution would kill everything. It was probably assumed that the waste would be diluted as it flowed downstream. Trust me, no one wanted to get in that river.

Our plan was to slide down the hill on a piece of cardboard. One of us would sit on the cardboard, another guy would give a shove, and the rider was flying down the steep grade at I'm sure was at least a hundred miles an hour. As the rider got close to the river, he would kick his heels through the ice to stop. It was a relatively simple process, and as a safety precaution, we created a snow barrier about fifteen feet from the river to stop us if the kick through the ice didn't work. Young boys, a plan, a steep hill, and a river. What could go wrong?

We were having a great time and things were going well—until it was Tom's turn to slide. Tom's speed was out of control, and his attempts to stop by digging into the ice were having no effect. As fate, or devious intentions, would have it, John was stationed as the safety net next to the snow barrier, and he had no intention of getting in the path of his speeding brother. So, of course, Tom continued sliding downhill right into the icy, nasty Blackstone River. We thought it was hysterical and continued to laugh as we pulled Tom out of the cold, rancid water. Fortunately, he only went in up to his waist. We grabbed his arms and pulled him out to land like a beached whale. Tom was not amused. He caught his breath, immediately tackled John, and tried to throw him into the river. We stopped Tom's river toss but let them fight it out in the snow.

In those days, when you did something wrong, you got punished. Sometimes we got caught (and it was easily done) because the neighbors would often tell on us. The usual punishment was being grounded for a week or so. Neighbors would surely tell on kids who were skipping school. Therefore, we couldn't go back to anyone's house in the middle of the day because we were supposed to be in school. Going to the "Y" was out of the question because employees would also tell on us. So, we had to think of a place we could go to hide, get warm, dry out soggy Tom, and not get in trouble. After much discussion, we decided on the post office.

The post office was on South Main Street, a block away from the YMCA. There was an area in the back, around the corner from the lobby, that was away from the counters and foot traffic. We spent three extremely long hours sitting there on the cold floor or standing by the bulletin board reading FBI Wanted posters. Tom stood next to the radiator trying to get dry. Every few minutes, he would step away from the heater just long enough to whack John.

Tom had to constantly be reminded to be quiet so we wouldn't get caught and thrown out. We couldn't dare go home for lunch. We had to stay there until school let out and we could then safely go to the Y. Once we got to the

Y, we put our clothes in the sauna to dry, headed for the shower room, and turned on all the hot water taps to create a steam bath to finally get the chill out of our wet bodies. Getting away with yet another adventure also warmed us. Tom, however, was still well beyond warm and continued to yell at and whack John. Ah, brotherly love.

FYI—David Stanley Jacubanis, a bank robber and member of the FBI's Most Wanted list, was caught in nearby North Smithfield.

Pack of Lies

John was built lean like his father, and like his father, he could run like the wind. It was said that when Mr. Wikiera was in the Army, he ran the hundred-yard dash in eleven seconds wearing a full backpack. Years later, in high school, I saw John run the hundred-yard dash in ten seconds flat from a football stance on a cinder track. The boy was damn fast. The only thing faster than John's feet was his mouth. It was that quick acid-like tongue and that "I didn't do anything wrong; you're picking on me" attitude that quite often started trouble and, in this case, got us suspended from the YMCA for two weeks.

It was a rainy Saturday afternoon and we had nothing to do. We killed a couple of hours watching *The Three Stooges* and then the Patriots on TV (the AFL played on Saturday afternoons while the NFL owned Sunday afternoons), but we were bored and needed some physical activity. We usually didn't mind playing football or anything else in the rain, but this was one of those miserable, wet, raw, New England days that kept everyone inside.

Suddenly, John broke the silence. "Why don't we go to the Y and shoot some hoops?" We all perked up.

I said, "Great idea, but the Y closes at 3:00 on Saturday afternoons and it's 3:30 now."

Most kids would have given up right then and there. But John said, "Haven't you noticed that when we go up the stairs from the locker room to the gym, the door to the alley isn't always locked?" We looked at each other and nodded, because it was open more times than it was locked. "What if we go down there and the door isn't locked? If the door is unlocked, then is the Y really closed?" It was an interesting theory. One which we all felt should be tested.

So, we walked through the windy, rainy weather to the Y. We checked the front door first, and of course, it was locked. Around the corner and down the alley was the six-foot-high wooden fence with a locked gate. Kevin lost the "who's going over the fence first" argument. We hoisted him up and over the fence to check the door, and fortunately, the door was unlocked. The rest of us climbed over the fence and our private playground was open for business.

"Wow, our own private gym," I said. "Where should we start? We can play anything we want!"

We began with two-on-two basketball—the usual teams of John and Kevin vs. Tom and me. They had finesse, we had strength; they were quick, we were brutal; they could shoot, we could rebound. Our totally different styles produced a competitive game. Our games were always close and this one was no different. When you're running the entire court (it wasn't regulation, only about a sixty-foot court) and the game is close, two things happen: you get tired and you get irritable. Kevin had just driven by me and scored. I wasn't going to let that happen again. But Kevin figured that if it worked once, why not try it again. As Kevin tried to go by me, I was ready. A well-placed forearm to the chest knocked him down.

"Foul!" screamed Kevin.

"I hardly touched you. If you can't take it, play ping-pong."

Tom called Kevin a puss, John threw the ball at Tom,

and the battle began. Basketball turned into dodgeball (a banned activity today) and it looked like a Keystone Cops chase scene with balls flying all over the place and no one getting hit. Dodgeball is a great game; it promotes agility, throwing, catching, and the opportunity to drill someone in the head. Because our three weapons of convenience were basketballs, no one was getting hit. We needed balls that were easier to throw. It so happened that, like the alley door, the equipment room was also unlocked. We now had twenty volleyball missiles to launch at each other. Kevin hit me; Tom and I drilled John at the same time, knocking him down. While he was down, we hit him again, and because he was a sitting duck, Kevin hit him too. There is little loyalty when such a great target of opportunity presents itself. John called a timeout to halt the pummeling.

It was a good time to take a break. The soda fountain was open, so we had a couple of cokes and began to plan the next activity. Kevin's eyes went bright, and he sported a big grin. "Let's have a slam-dunk contest."

That's right, four guys with an average height of five foot three were going to get the springboard out of the equipment room and sky like the pros. Actually, at that time, there were no fancy dunks; the pros dunked the ball to score, not to make a highlight reel. ESPN with *SportsCenter* was years away, so there were no nightly highlights. It was the American Basketball Association (ABA) that started the slam-dunk contest during their all-star break in 1976 with one of the first acrobatic dunkers, Julius Erving a.k.a. Dr. J.

The springboard launched us much higher than we could jump on our own, which meant that the landing was a lot farther down. The walls of the gym were covered with gray, four-by-eight-foot mats. To counter the steeper drop, we stripped the walls and piled the mats high enough under the basket to look like a big gray elephant. With the "elephant" under the basket and the spring-board, we could sky and dunk like Dr. J or Michael Jordan (neither were playing yet, but I can't think of any good slam-dunkers from that time period). The contest began with the standard two-handed, straight-on dunk and pro-gressed to the spinning 360 followed by the alley-oop. Five feet tall and slamming the ball better than Bill Russell or Wilt "the Stilt" Chamberlain; damn we were good.

It was getting late, so we painstakingly put everything away in its proper place. No one would ever be the wiser about our closed-gym activities.

Wow! What a day. It started out cold and miserable and ended with warm feelings and big smiles. We played bas-ketball, dodgeball, slam-dunked, and drank a few cokes. We showered, turned the lights off, and headed for home, tired but content. Mission accomplished! A fantastic day!

However, as with every "too good to be true" oppor-tunity, there was a downside. The YMCA had a dormitory on the top floor. We had been completely oblivious to the men, referred to as the boarders, who lived there. While some of the boarders became fans who enjoyed watching us, there were a few who objected to our Saturday games and reported us to the director, who on Monday, called us into his office to face the charges.

"What are we going to say?" Tom asked. "I hope we don't get thrown out or suspended from the basketball league." That was a real concern because our team, the Fossils, was in first place. We had lumps in our throats as we walked into the director's office. Mr. Georges was a quiet, soft-spoken man. We liked him and felt that he liked us too.

"Sit down, boys," he softly said as we entered the room. "I understand you had a pretty good time here Saturday afternoon after we closed." While we sat there squirming, he went down the list of our alleged infractions. We were blamed for many things we didn't do, like throwing food around the gym, excessive swearing (yes, we did swear, but not excessively) and yelling, and not leaving when told to leave. None of those things happened, but those were the charges levied against us by the boarders.

"What do you have to say for yourselves?" We sat around the conference table with our heads down, trying to look contrite while justifying our actions. It's hard to come up with valid excuses when you know that the locked front door meant that the Y was closed, and we were wrong. But using the logic of twelve-year-olds, we tried to explain how an unlocked door meant that the Y was really open for business. It was an impossible sell, but we tried, and I think we were doing okay; we were polite, remorseful, and thought we had a chance of avoiding the devastating two-week suspension.

Finally, Director Georges looked at us and again asked, "What do you have to say for yourselves?"

Tom, Kevin, and I mumbled a little about being sorry, but didn't really say anything. John always had a different way of looking at things. He believed that if you weren't caught "red-handed" then you weren't really caught at all. He also believed that if something wasn't 100 percent true then it wasn't true at all. He stood up, looked Mr. Georges straight in the eye, and said, "It's all a pack of lies."

"You're out!" screamed the once soft-spoken director. "Don't come back for two weeks!"

On the way out the door, we yelled at John, and Tom knocked him down with a good whack to the back of the head. When John got up, he pushed Tom and, naturally, a fight broke out, a fight that had two weeks to work itself out.

Robby Rabbit

Robby was a funny little guy we called Robby Rabbit because of his big buck teeth. He was harmless and liked by everyone. Robby was in a special class, which today would be comprised of "special needs" students or "differently abled" clients. But back then we would just say that he was retarded. Actually, in the Boston-area vernacular, he would have been called "wicked, freakin' retarded." By today's standards, we were politically incorrect bullies to utter a banned, insensitive word such as *retarded*, but the social justice warriors and language police had yet to start their assault on the United States Constitution and the First Amendment; so, we were boorish but not criminal.

Robby Rabbit was an avid Red Sox fan who could quote every statistic for every player. He listened to every Sox game through the static on his AM radio and was our go-to source for Sox info. His favorite player was the Red Sox left fielder Carl Yastrzemski—better known as "Yaz" by anyone who knew baseball at all, not just loyal Sox fans. Such devotion made Robby okay with us.

Woonsocket is a small city that was originally divided into villages, each of which retained some unique personality. Social was known for its blue-collar tough guys. One day, Robby Rabbit had a little bit of trouble with some of the tough guys from Social. Our school was on its own block with the Hamlet Avenue Bridge crossing the Blackstone River on one side, heading toward Social; on the other side was the footbridge that we used to cross the railroad tracks to get us toward the North End. We didn't actually have "turf" like the Sharks and the Jets claimed in *West Side Story* (we couldn't dance or sing, either), but the Social boys were definitely not in their part of town. Bobby, apparently a big shot in Social, and two of his cronies were picking on Robby—knocking his books out of his hands, pushing him around, and generally giving him a hard time just because he was a goofy, bucktooth, funny little guy, and an easy mark.

As Tom and I were crossing the footbridge on our way home, we saw what the gutless bullies were doing to defenseless Robby Rabbit. Granted, we sometimes gave him a hard time, but he was our friend and we decided we had to help. Though we teased him some, we never touched him and weren't about to let these reprobates do it, either—in the classic "I can talk bad about my mother, but I'll kick your ass if you do" mentality.

Tom and I confronted the three guys from Social. We told them to stop, which only generated some laughs and the inevitable "What are you going to do about it?" Being outnumbered, we weren't exactly looking for a fight, but we stepped between Robby Rabbit and the Social boys anyway and told them to back off. They made the incorrect assumption that because there were three of them, we would back down. Actually, because of their reputation for being tough guys, they were *sure* we would back down. But we didn't. They began to push and shove us. They were surprised when we pushed and shoved back a lot harder than they expected. We stood our ground. They hesitated a few seconds and moved back. They weren't used to having anyone stand up to them, especially when they had an advantage in numbers. We held our ground and they stopped. Heated words were exchanged, none of which our parents or priests would condone; but the physical confrontation was over, and Robby Rabbit was okay. Though we never got into an actual fistfight, we were ready, and the Social goons left with some respect for us. Remember the great Beach Boys' song "I Get Around"? They sang of bad guys backing down to good guys. Well, after this encounter, the "bad guys" found out that we were not just park league athletes who could take hits, but also that we never backed down. Bobby and his guys headed back across the bridge toward Social and never bothered Robby or us again. Looks like strength in numbers isn't all it's cracked up to be after all.

By the way, none of us were sent to anger-management classes or empathy training.

Poison Sumac

It was going to be a glorious May day in Woonsocket. We only had three weeks before school would be out for the summer, but this day was too perfect to waste sitting in class. The average high for May was sixty-eight degrees, but on this day the temperature would be up to seventy-five. School would have to wait. We couldn't allow a beautiful day like this to be wasted. Using today's term and logic, this was a mental health day.

John, Tom, Obie, and I decided that we would take the day off and go swimming. Getchell's, Harris Pond, and Social Ocean were out of the question; too many people would see us and report we bunked school. Why skipping school was called bunking, I don't know, but that's what it was called back then. We had to find a place to go and get moving before someone saw us. John had an idea: the limestone quarry.

Just south of Woonsocket on Route 146, the main highway between Woonsocket and Providence, was a limestone quarry. There were trees all around it and on the left side was a huge rock. Some said it was fifty feet high and we believed it. Truth be told, it was maybe twenty feet, but whether it was twenty or fifty feet high didn't matter. The challenge was to leap from the top.

We mounted our bikes and rode about five miles to the quarry. Once we got there, we followed the path through the woods to the base of the big rock and the mythical bottomless pond below it. The only thing we brought with us was enthusiasm. Because we were truant, we didn't bring bathing suits or towels. So skinny-dipping it would be.

Off came the clothes and up the path we ran through the leaves and bushes. The big rock had multiple ledges to jump from before we got to the legendary fifty-foot level. We stopped at the ten-foot spot and then proceeded into the who-would-go-first discussion. This was standard procedure. Before we slid down the hill toward the Blackstone River, we had to discuss it. Before we swung on the Tarzan swing at Getchell's and let go into the lake, we had to discuss it. Before we did anything, there was the back-and-forth talking then yelling about who would go first, and it ended the same way every time. Tom would yell, "Shut up, I'll go."

Tom took a deep breath and took the plunge into the bottomless pit. That was the other part of the legend; the pond was bottomless. After decades of limestone excavation, it truly was very deep, deeper than we could dive. We stared at the pond until Tom broke the surface wearing nothing but a big smile. That was the signal for the rest of us to make the leap. We jumped from various heights until we got to the top, where Tom took the leap before we even got into the who-would-go-first talk.

When we reached the summit, we were visible to the road. Most of the people speeding on Route 146 were heading south to Providence or north to Woonsocket and never noticed us. Most drivers didn't see us, but two men did. Those two men happened to be Lincoln policemen. They yelled for us to come down and get dressed. We were asked the usual questions about who we were, where we lived, etc. But the whole time they were laughing. Obie finally asked, "What's so funny?"

They responded that we were running through poison sumac and would soon be itching like crazy. John sarcastically told them that because we weren't allergic to poison ivy, we probably were immune to poison sumac. They continued to laugh and told us to get going.

Tom, Obie, and I had a baseball game that evening, so we headed for home to change into our baseball uniforms. Unfortunately for us, the cops were right. We were miserable, itching and scratching like crazy from the neck down. Neck down means *everything* from the neck down. Our heavy wool uniforms made the itching more intense. And scratching became the priority, not catching the ball. Bunking school was never worth this misery.

The Coasters, a sixties singing group, had a hit song called "Poison Ivy" that suggested it's going to take a boatful of calamine lotion to reduce our itching and irritation. No truer words were ever penned. We needed every drop of that magic, soothing lotion.

The fight that broke out this time was with Ma Nature— and she won big time.

Banana Ball

Ah, spring! The snow finally has melted, the grass miraculously has changed from dormant brown to emerald green, and the air smells sweet. Whereas proverbially young boys' thoughts turn to fancy, our thoughts turned to bikes, baseball, and fishing.

As soon as ice began to melt, whether it was after school or on weekends, we could be found on the little league field at Cold Spring Park. It was a typical little league field surrounded by a chain-link fence with center field 250 feet from home plate. Beyond the outfield was a jungle of weeds, bushes, and briars so thick that a person could hardly walk through it. Since the season hadn't started, the field was usually available for us to play pickup games. Though we preferred to play a full baseball game with nine players on each side, it was generally impossible to get eighteen guys together. Necessity is indeed the mother of invention, and since we seldom had the necessary numbers, we had to invent different varieties of the game. The number of people who showed up dictated the type of game that we would play that day. Keep in mind that we were playing in a time before parents organized "playdates" or sought intervention from the internet in order to entertain children. We were left to our own devices and imagination, and always managed to find a solution to any obstacles to our plans.

We almost always played a variation on the same theme, a game we called "Banana Ball." Banana Ball required a minimum of five players. Each team would have a shortstop and a left fielder, since, as genetic luck would have it, everyone batted right-handed. The fifth person would pitch to both teams, cover first base, and umpire. Any ball hit to right field was an automatic out. A fly ball that dropped in the outfield was a double, and if the ball hit the fence on a fly it was a triple. Every grounder had to be run out. If the ball went through the infield, it was a single. If the shortstop played the ball and threw the ball to the pitcher covering first, the runner was out. A runner safe at first would become a shadow runner while the batter went back to take his place in the hitting order. As hits occurred, the shadow runners advanced automatically around the bases to score runs. Amazingly—unlike players in today's MLB—none of us had to wear cheat sheets on our forearms or in our ball caps to keep up with the complexities of the game.

It didn't matter whether we were playing a full roster game or Banana Ball, when the teams were finally drawn up, Tom and John were always on opposing teams. The rivalry of brothers can be a beautiful thing. Playing on different teams was just an extension of their antagonism at home.

So, it was on one fateful early spring day when Tom and I played against John and Kevin while Obie pitched. Anytime Obie was involved with anything, there was controversy. He knew what everyone's buttons were and was an expert at pushing them, especially Tom's. It never mattered to Obie what the consequences would be when tormenting Tom; he just counted on there being some because Tom was bigger, stronger, and didn't like it when someone "got his ass."

This was a game that amounted to three on two, since

every time there was a close call, Obie, in a supposedly impartial position, would side with John and Kevin. Such allegiance was pretty typical, and Tom and I had learned to live with it. Our acquiescence didn't sit well with Obie; he always had to push things in order to provoke a response. This particular game was a close one. Shadow runners were flying around the bases. John hit a grounder to Tom at short. He gobbled up the ball and threw it to Obie at first, who proceeded to intentionally drop it. John was safe. Not only did Obie drop the ball, but the error was also followed by his familiar trademark sneer that provoked Tom's immediate swell of anger. Obie's well-planned error started the inevitable argument.

"Obie dropped it on purpose!" Tom screamed. "You're out!"

"No way!" chimed Kevin and John. "It was a bad throw. He dropped the ball. If the first baseman drops the ball, you're safe. You didn't drop it on purpose, did you, Obie?"

"Me? Me?" Obie yelled in his defense. "I tried to catch it, but it wasn't a good throw and it curved like hell. Maybe it curved because Tom is a sorry left-handed short-stop and his sidearm throw has a natural curve." Well, that last excuse didn't sit well with Tom. Yes, he was left-handed and threw hard, but Obie was an exceptionally good player who rarely had a problem catching the ball, no matter where it was thrown or by whom.

It didn't take long for Tom to get even. The very next inning, John came up to the plate and hit a screaming grounder through the infield. He didn't expect me to charge the ball, so he took his sweet time going to first base. I picked up the ball and flipped it to Tom at short-stop. He turned toward first and saw that John, instead of running past first base, had made the turn toward second and was leisurely strolling back to first. Tom reared back and unleashed a rocket. The stingray hit John right in the back of the head and knocked him out cold before he could get back to first base.

"Now you're out!" Tom said with conviction.

You might think that Kevin, Obie, and I would have been panicking and running to help John, but our calm response was a testament to the fact that everyone knew that something memorable was just about to happen. The only unknown was the degree to which it would escalate.

When John woke up and could finally see through the haze . . . of course, a fight broke out.

That day at the ball field was thoroughly enjoyed by everyone. Well, maybe not so much by John. Tom was happy because he got his revenge, whacked his brother, and sent a message to all. I was happy that I was always on Tom's team and that we had won that game. Kevin was happy that it was John and not he who took the shot to the head. And then there was Obie, who was ecstatic that he had found another opportunity to get Tom's ass and create utter chaos within the group. It never mattered to Obie what the subject was, only that there was a shot to "stick in a knife and twist." What he didn't realize was that this time, he had stuck Tom once too often and twisted the knife one time too many.

That night, there was a little league game between Fairmount Post and Nyanza Mills. Tom was scheduled to pitch for the Post and Obie was playing shortstop and batting second for Nyanza. Tom gained a valuable insight when his stingray hit John in the back of the head that morning while playing Banana Ball; he liked doing it! He got even, got his point across, and it felt good. Just before the game and throughout the warm-up, Tom and Obie traded glares and trash talk. Not everyone there that evening knew what was coming, but Tom and Obie surely did. Nyanza was up first. As the first batter, Ray Thompson, stepped up to the plate, he looked scared. Tom was left-handed, fast, and known to be wild on his better days. Tom, who either couldn't, or wouldn't, hide his emotions, had a particularly strange look on his face, which added to the batter's trepidation. What Ray didn't know was that Tom couldn't wait to get to Obie and that the fastest way to get to Obie was to get him in the batter's box. And to Tom's way of thinking, the fastest way to get the batter in the box out of the way was to hit Ray.

The leadoff hitter is usually a good athlete, quick and agile, as was the case with Nyanza's. He managed to avoid the first pitch. However, not even his inherent talent could avoid Tom's second pitch, which caught him dead in the ribs. He thankfully took first base. Next up was the object of Tom's anger. The look on Tom's face told Obie everything he needed to know. He took an unusually long time stepping into the batter's box. Before Tom could pitch, Obie stepped out of the box in an effort to delay the inevitable, or possibly to give Tom a chance to change his mind about what Obie, and now most of both benches, was pretty sure was going to happen. Obie stepped back into the box but never even had a chance to lift the bat. As Tom wound up to deliver the first pitch, Obie winced. To his credit, he managed to turn quickly and took his punishment in the middle of the back.

With runners now on first and second, it was the third hitter's turn to bat. There were tears in Billy Smith's eyes and his knees were knocking as he stepped in. A footprint couldn't be found in the batter's box. Tom realized that this intimidation game was fun, and that third base was open. In those days, pitchers were rarely given warnings, much less taken out of games for a few errant throws. The fact that Tom's father was the coach may also have helped keep Tom on the mound. So, batter number three became the next notch on Tom's glove. With the bases loaded and nobody out, it looked like quite a predicament. At that point, Tom could have pitched underhand and no one would have taken a cut at the ball. They needed diapers to catch the crap in their pants. The next three batters never took the bat off their shoulders and went down on called strikes. Tom enjoyed yet another "thrill of victory."

Regardless of where or with whom we played, or whether it was an organized game or Banana Ball, we were equipment challenged. Unlike kids today, we didn't wear two-hundreddollar sunglasses backward on our caps or carry monogrammed bat bags with four-hundred-dollar bats inside. Our bats were made of wood. When our wooden Louisville Slugger bats cracked, we repaired them with screws (if we could find some) and black electrical tape. Consequently, losing anything would cause financial stress as well as game delay. At twelve years old, we were able and proud to hit home runs over the 250-foot fence. Ironically, the euphoria that accompanied the long ball was short-lived when the reality sank in that we had to find the ball in the aforementioned impassable jungle beyond.

Such was the case one day when Kevin drove the ball deep over the left-field fence. Kevin and John's elation over "going yard" and Tom's and my disappointment soon gave way to blank stares and the inevitable argument. Who was going to search for the ball? While Kevin and John contended Tom and I were closer to the ball, the fact was that

Kevin hit it. The dispute ended when Obie, rarely the voice of reason, pointed out that it was our last ball. It was rare that we had the luxury of having an extra ball. So, in desperation, everyone went over the fence. After an exhaustive search and bloody scratches, we finally gave up. As we sat there wondering where we could get another ball, Kevin said that he thought that he had one at home. We all hopped on our bikes and rode—without helmets or knee pads—to his house. After searching through the mess that was his room, we came up empty. On the way out, passing through the living room, we noticed that there on the mantel—in this case, an appropriate place—sat baseballs, lots of baseballs. Kevin's uncle was an umpire in the American League and had given Kevin's father a complete set of baseballs autographed by the 1961 New York Yankees. Among the autographed balls were ones signed by Mickey Mantle, Whitey Ford, Roger Maris, and a ball signed by the entire 1961 team. We stood in awe in the presence of baseballs signed by the players of arguably the greatest team in the history of baseball. Yes, we were Red Sox fans, but the Yankees did win a lot of championships. After we all held and read the names on the baseballs, Kevin picked up one and said, "Yogi Berra, he's only a catcher. Let's go."

We beat that ball until Yogi's name was illegible. And when the seams tore and the cover was ready to fall off, we taped it up and continued to hit it. And then it went the way of its predecessors, lost over the fence, never to be seen again. Kevin's father, Woonsocket's chief of police, had to deal with dirtbags and miscreants all day. When he arrived home, he was less than a happy man when he discovered that his son was a petty thief and Yogi was missing from the mantel. Details are unknown, but we didn't see Kevin for a while after that.

Carrying the Worms

Getchell's Lake was an idyllic spot in rural Massachusetts, just over the border from Woonsocket. Tom Sawyer and Huck Finn had the Mississippi, we had Getchell's. While it wasn't the biggest lake around, what it offered us was enormous.

There was a small beach area for swimming and a lot of openings around the lake's border from which we could step into the water and fish. Off to the right, just above the dam, was the Staples family farm. The kids who lived there built a raft out of old pieces of wood and inner tubes. We became friends and they allowed us to use the raft for exploring, fishing, roughhousing, and lounging. There were three ways to get to the raft. One was to walk back to the road, cross the bridge, then walk about two hundred yards to the farm. Too far, too long, and no excitement. The second was to swim seventy-five yards to the raft. Not a long swim, but it was against the current, which made it challenging though doable. Our third option took some courage. We could walk across the dam. The lake water flowed over the dam and dropped ten feet to the shallow, rocky stream below, making this treacherous yet exciting. Naturally, this was our preferred route.

Just past the parking lot on the lake bank was a tall oak tree with a Tarzan swing. It wasn't exactly the Tarzan swing in the cloud forest of Monteverde, Costa Rica, with a height of 148 feet and a length 294 feet. It was about a 30-foot swing, but to us, very scary and fun. All you had to do was grab the rope, run toward the lake, and jump on the big knot at the bottom of the rope. When you swung back toward the shore, the other guys would give you a push to gain more height. Then, at the peak of the swing, you'd let go into the lake. I don't know how many times I rode the swing, but letting go and flying into the lake was a rush every time.

Fishing requires poles, bait, and lures. Getting bait took planning. On damp evenings, we would go out to the North End, sneak on people's beautifully manicured lawns, and pick up night crawlers. Other times, we would dig for worms. On rare occasions, if we had a little money, we would go to a bait shop and chip in to buy a dozen shiners. Our last resort and most difficult method of acquiring live bait was to bait small hooks with bread and catch shiners below the dam at Getchell's.

Whether it was worms or shiners, getting the bait to our destination was always a bone of contention. Bicycles were our primary means of transportation and took us all over Woonsocket and the surrounding areas. SUVs had yet to be invented and our parents, unlike parents of today, didn't view themselves as our transportation coordinators. We had three-speed, English-style bikes that required two hands to use the brakes, so no one wanted to carry the bait. However, Tom didn't need his hands to stop his bike, since the brakes didn't work. So, even though every time we went fishing, there would be an argument about who would carry the worms or shiners, Tom would always—and logically, so we thought—lose the vote, 3-1. He would claim it wasn't fair (remind you of any recent elections?) and the argument would start again. Finally, John would say that he didn't need worms anyway, he would fish with lures, at which he was very adept. Kevin and I would agree, and that left Tom with the worms because he didn't have any lures. He could either carry the worms or not fish. Tom begrudgingly grabbed the bait and off we went.

As soon as we got to our fishing destination, John would be John and immediately grab a worm from Tom and bait his hook. Tom would seethe. He was never able to hide his anger very well, which delighted John. Our goal was to catch a big bass. In the Woonsocket area, catching an eight-pound largemouth bass would get your picture in the *Woonsocket Call*. None of us ever caught anything close to that size. But in our eyes, catching any size bass was a big deal and we thought a two-pound bass was huge. Really, catching anything was great because we seldom fished for very long.

Bass fishing can be boring. Step one, bait the hook. Step two, set the float at about eighteen inches. Step three, cast your line into the lake. Step four, sit and wait, hoping there will be a step five, reel in a fish. Before we ever had a chance to catch anything, John would get antsy and toss small pebbles into the water. It wasn't his intent to disrupt the fishing but more of an involuntary act of boredom. This lull in activity prompted Tom to start on John about using the worms that he had refused to carry. He started with the typical verbal abuse and moved on to throwing small rocks at John's float. No big rocks were thrown, just big enough to scare the fish away and piss off John. John responded by escalating the fishing disruption. Well, the next rock came from Tom and he aimed it at John's float. John retaliated with another rock aimed at Tom's float. Then, of course, they would start to throw bigger and bigger rocks at each other's float. Kevin and I knew the drill. We laughed as we reeled in our lines.

As you can guess, bass fishing was over for the day. John and Tom threw a bunch of punches at each other with neither landing many scoring blows. Lots of shots to the arms and legs with an occasional punch to the gut. A few more punches were thrown followed by a lot of expletives, and then it was time to move on. We'd head off to swim and play on the Tarzan swing, where Tom would inevitably swing out immediately after John in an attempt to land on him. Yep, round two.

INTERMEDIATE MEMBERS

. . . These lads compete for the YMCA in the Intermediate Basketball League. Kneeling from left, Doug Brooks and John Wikiera; standing, Tom Wikiera, Paul Dubois.

A spectacular catch by Farrow for T.D.

Bob Farrow

Doug Brooks leaps high in the air to tip the ball away in the Cumberland game.

Willie Barr

John Wilkins jumps high in the air looking over the hands of Classical defenders for a receiver.

KEV LYNCH   JIMMY O'BRIEN

Tom and John

In Barrington Game, Tom Wikiera
dashes to a sizeable gain.

COLD SPRING VOLLEYBALL CHAMPS

. . . Top men in the 14-16 year-old volleyball class at the Woonsocket playgrounds are, front, from left, Doug Brooks, ████████, Tom Wikiera, Al Durand, ████████ ████████ and Kevin Lynch; rear, John Wikiera, ████████,

MEET THE VOLLEYBALL CHAMPS

Cold Spring won the playground volleyball championship. Personnel, ████████ from left, John Wikiera, Al Durand, Kevin Lynch and Doug Brooks; ████████ Supervisor Al Wade, Carl Kwoulka, Tom Wikiera and Duke Dubois.

Doug and Tom

John, Obie, Kevin, Tom, and Doug

Post Office

John and Doug

Recognition

Generally, in whatever activity we were engaged, we wanted to get our pictures in the *Woonsocket Call*. When we went fishing, we wanted to catch an eight-pound bass. In whatever sport we were playing, we wanted to win the league, city, or state championship so we would get our pictures in the newspaper. Fortunately, those were goals that, eventually, all of us achieved. Cameras at that time were rarely accessible, and if your parents had one there was no way they were going to trust you with it. Consequently, among all of us, there were few pictures that we have of ourselves other than those in the newspaper.

One afternoon around dusk, Tom, Duke (Paul Dubois, another close friend of ours), Obie, and I were walking home from Cold Spring Park. We decided to take the long way and traveled through the very wealthy section of Woonsocket in the North End adjacent to the park. We had several good friends who were lucky enough to live in such a nice neighborhood. We enjoyed seeing the great homes with their beautifully landscaped manicured lawns and running through the backyards, creating a little havoc along the way. Few people—not even the wealthy—had clothes dryers; laundry was hung outside on a clothesline. There was a line full of clothes flapping in the breeze in the backyard we were cutting through. The owners' small dog was outside as usual, but since he was familiar with us, he didn't bark and pretty much ignored us. Obie, infamous for spontaneous, often ill-thought, endeavors, spied a bra hanging on the line and had the bright idea of putting it on the dog. The fifty-five-pound retriever mix sporting a lacy double-D bra not only made us laugh, but also whetted our appetite for doing something even more entertaining.

We continued our walk down Meadow Road, past a house with a big "For Sale" sign in front of it. Once again, we noticed that Obie had "that look" in his eyes, which meant he had come up with yet another crazy plan. Sure enough he blurted out, "Let's take this sign and put it in front of that mansion"—we called it Sid's castle—"at the end of the street." We all smiled and agreed that this was a brilliant idea. Obie and I orchestrated the move while Duke and Tom did the heavy lifting. We ran as fast as we could and worked quickly to secure the "For Sale" sign in front of the big house. As we ran away, we took great pride in our accomplishment and talked about the look sure to be on the owner's face the next morning when he saw that his home was for sale.

Imagine our astonishment when the next day in the evening paper, there was a big picture of the house with the sign in front of it and the headline "Not for Sale!" The text below explained that the owner of the home, a prominent local businessman, awoke to phone calls from neighbors and friends asking why he was selling his home and buyers interested in his magnificent property. It went on to say that when he looked outside and saw the sign, he started to laugh.

We loved that our trick worked out better than we could ever have imagined. Although we did not get our pictures or names in the paper, we took great satisfaction in how our actions were perceived by the owner and covered by the press. We were especially glad for the recognition we did NOT receive!

The Three-Dollar Lure

Fishing was one of our passions, so figuring out better methods of catching fish was often on our minds. Some methods proved to be great adventures for young boys. Digging worms, going to the mansions in the North End at night with flashlights after the lawns were watered to pick up large night crawlers, and using bread to catch shiners in a stream to use to catch bass and pickerel in a lake or pond, which, when dissected and bloody, would attract even bigger fish, were all easily accomplished. However, our search for the perfect lure rivaled nothing short of Herculean.

Although comic books were our first choice in fine literature, magazines dealing with fishing were definitely a close second. We would read them on the sly from the rack in Almac's Supermarket and attempt to commit to memory techniques and bait that the experts used to catch "the big ones." It was in one of these magazines that Tom saw an ad for the Vivif. He was mainly a worm and shiner fisherman but was more than a little intrigued by this amazing lure. Never had he lusted for something with such fervor. The Vivif was magnificent and way ahead of its time. It was heavier than most lures, had a metal head, a body and tail that were soft plastic, and vibrated and moved exactly like a real fish. It was guaranteed to catch fish, and for the exorbitant price of three dollars, it surely ought to. Money was tough for a twelve-year-old in the early sixties. Allowances were unheard of (who paid a kid for doing chores?), and parents' handouts were even rarer. Tommy worked hard for the money he saved and was loathe to spend it. But he was determined to buy the Vivif fishing lure. He dipped into his snow-shoveling money and bit the bullet. He was beyond proud. He talked incessantly about the eight-pound largemouth bass (known as lunkers) that he was going to catch, and couldn't wait for the day that he could cast his lure into action.

That day finally arrived. He, John, Kevin, and I made our way to Harris Pond, a large pond that had been an enormous lake before Hurricane Carol broke through the dam and flooded a large portion of Woonsocket. Reliable rumors swore that vestiges of the lake's huge fish still lived in the pond. As usual, Tom started the day using worms, waiting to use his "guarantee" for just the right moment. John, who was particularly talented at catching fish on lures, decided Tom's Vivif was the best-looking lure that he had ever seen. Sneakily borrowing Tom's best and favorite things without asking was a habit of John's, one at which he was quite adept. So, he waited and watched until Tom moved off to a point just down the bank with his back to the others. What an opportunity! John grabbed the lure and quickly attached it to his swivel. As John reached back to cast the lure *way out there*, Tom turned around just in time to see the heavy lure snap the line at the apex of the cast. The lure flew, unattached, about ninety feet to the deepest part of the pond. Kevin and I were unsympathetically, but understandably, roaring. For what seemed like an eternity, Tom and John just stared at each other in amazement and horror before the action began. John was quick, but with the water on one side and thick briars on the other, it didn't take long for Tom to catch him. Wow, did a fight ever break out! It didn't take long for the fight to move from the shore to the pond. The fact that they were both completely soaked when they finally tired of flailing at each other merely added amusement for us bystanders. For the rest of that summer, and for two years after, Tom would drag me to that historical site in order to dive into the murky water to look for his favorite lure, the one he coveted and paid dearly for and never even got to use. Alas, unlike the current generation of parents, Tom's never consoled him by replacing his lure (which, by the way, now lists online for forty-eight dollars).

Hook to the Head

Getchell's Lake was the best place in the world for us to fish, swim, and generally mess around. It was much more than just a fishing hole; it was like a huge playground offering us a variety of activities. There was bass and pickerel fishing in the lake above the dam and trout fishing in the stream below, plus a great rope swing for anytime the weather was hot and the fishing was not. If we wanted a fishing trip and an adventure, we could get on our big inner tubes and float downstream from Getchell's to another prime fishing spot, Harris Pond, about a mile away. The waters from Harris Pond fed the manmade swimming pond at World War II Memorial State Park in Woonsocket. Because the name of the village in which the park was located was "Social," it came to be known as "Social Ocean."

From Cold Spring Place to Getchell's wasn't more than five miles, and we usually rode our bikes. But on this particular day, Mr. and Mrs. Wikiera gave us a ride in their 1961 Ford Falcon. For those not familiar with the Falcon, it was a six-passenger car that provided plenty of room for three skinny young boys and their fishing gear. As I said, it may have been a short ride, but rarely was that trip uneventful. We were in the back seat holding our fishing poles; Tom sat on the left, myself in the middle, and John on the right. I sat in the middle because John and Tom always needed a buffer. Short ride, a buffer, parents in the front seat—what could happen? Well, as always, there was some excitement. Tom screamed, "Stop the car. I hooked myself in the eye!" To a normal person, a fishhook in the eye would be a serious problem, but to John, it was hilarious. Mrs. Wikiera got excited; Mr. Wikiera calmly pulled off the road onto the dirt shoulder. And John could not stop laughing. Fortunately, Tom hadn't really hooked his eye; close, but the hook never really penetrated the skin, and as we pulled to a stop, the hook swung free. Tom stopped screaming, John continued laughing, and that started a fight as Tom climbed over me to whack John. This was to be the first fight for that day. John was still laughing, and Tom was firing verbal rockets while reaching over me to hit John. Mr. and Mrs. Wikiera were threatening to turn around if the boys didn't quiet down.

This was going to be a trout-fishing afternoon below the dam. We usually fished for trout in the morning, but Tom was anxious to try out his new fly rod. Having a fly rod made him feel superior and he felt that fly-fishing was a skill that could be mastered in a minimal amount of time. The fly rod really wasn't new; it was a hand-me-down from his Uncle Stash. Anyone who fly-fishes knows that the flies are supposed to be on the surface and the line is supposed to float. Tom's line didn't float. Add to the sinking line the fact that, other than watching Gadabout Gaddis on a local TV fishing show, Tom had no clue how to fly-fish. But how hard could it be?

John and I were using spinning reels with red-and-white-striped spoons called Daredevils. The Daredevil was a very versatile lure, great for trout fishing in the stream or bass and pickerel fishing in the lake. The rare trout we caught were just above the legal six inches long, but fun to catch. Just standing in a stream, casting our lines, and balancing on the wet, slippery rocks was a challenge.

Tom was whipping the fly back and forth with such seeming skill that to the untrained eye, he appeared to know what he was doing. With eyes straight ahead and no clue as to who or what was behind him, Tom would whip the fly back and forth while slowly letting the line out. John, who rarely paid attention to his surroundings, gradually drifted behind Tom, so it didn't take long for the inevitable: one of Tom's backcasts hooked John in the back of the head. John, with his flair for the dramatic, screamed like a banshee. Tom knew that he was stuck on something, and though he was a good math student, he couldn't put two and two together. So, he pulled harder and John screamed louder. After a couple of tugs, Tom turned around, looked at John, and laughed. With a little slack in the line, John got the hook out (it wasn't buried very deep), and he started toward Tom. He sloshed through the stream and tried to hit him with his pole. He missed, fell in the stream, and Tom and I howled.

Events can be remembered in different ways. Memories vary from each person's viewpoint. What was fun for one may have been pain for the other. Remember a few paragraphs back when Tom hooked himself in the eye? Well, paybacks are a bitch. Fight number two started in the stream and continued long after the loving brothers reached the shore.

Impulse

Riding our bikes was fun—they expanded our universe and they quickly got us where we wanted to go. There were, however, many times that we ended up walking. Walking anywhere with Obie along was usually an adventure. He was always an enigma. No one had a clue as to what was going through his mind or what he was going to say or do to any of us—or to any of the unsuspecting people we may encounter. The one constant was that whatever he did or said was certain to cause a problem, and the bigger the problem, the more he seemed to enjoy it. It was as if he were a Great White shark who could smell blood in the water and who delighted in the attack. He swore that many of his endeavors "just happened"; they were merely "impulsive acts." Obie was, if not certifiably nuts, on some "spectrum" of crazy. But his antics made him border on heroic to those to whom he, or we, relayed the often-embellished stories.

Such an adventure happened one summer evening when we were walking through the North End. We were going from Kevin's house to mine. To do so, we had to pass by the North Main Street Fire Station. A few of the firemen were sitting out front shooting the breeze on a warm, pleasant New England evening. As we passed by, about a hundred yards right in front of them, a telephone pole caught our attention. Attached to the pole was a fire alarm. I was in front of the others but stopped dead in my tracks when I heard Tom say, "Don't do it!" I turned around to see Obie looking at the alarm. Once again, Tom repeated, "Don't do it; they're looking right at us!"

That was all Obie needed to hear. The gauntlet was thrown; it was now a challenge he could not pass up. None of us even waited to see if his arm was going up because we knew that it was. Anticipating the inevitable, we took off in different directions. As I heard the screeching wail of the fire alarm, I took a quick look over my shoulder and saw the firemen jump off their chairs and make a beeline for us. The good news was that we knew every inch of the area, so John, Kevin, and Obie ran through backyards toward the homes that offered the biggest shrubs that could be used as hiding places. Tom and I headed toward the railroad tracks that were lined with a dense assortment of trees, shrubs, weeds and grasses, briars, and prickly pears. In a few minutes, the alarm quit blaring and the firemen decided that pursuing delinquents wasn't worth giving up some free time on a nice day.

We all met up about an hour later and spent the rest of the afternoon sharing our tales of harrowing escape and our versions of the exhilarating adventure. Tom and I bore the scratches, bruises, and remnants of thorns and prickly bushes hanging from our clothes as trophies of a success-ful escape. We all went home with smiles, having gotten away with one of the most brazen acts ever committed—at least in our adolescent, daredevil minds.

We were pretty well known in the community. In this case, notoriety had its price. It didn't help that Kevin's brother was a patrolman on the police force and his father was the chief of police. News—especially bad news—trav-els fast in small towns and all hell broke loose when Kevin got home. We didn't see him for what seemed a long time, during which he sat gingerly, recovering from a punishment we were glad we didn't experience. When he finally showed up again, Kevin glared at the perpetrator with a look that belied his usual docile, passive nature and impulsively proceeded to lay a fairly good beating on poor ol' Obie. Sadly, no repercussion daunted Obie's continued lifetime of impulsive misadventures.

Driving without a License

The Woonsocket YMCA had one of the best men's volleyball teams in the country. As adolescents, we had the opportunity to play with and learn from fantastic players who won the 1964 national championship. It was great being on the court with these men, but unlike the woke, sensitive men of today, they were not easy on us.

In our current promote-self-esteem culture, twelve- and thirteen-year-old boys competing with grown men would receive nothing but superlative praise, no matter how poorly they played. "Good job; nice try; great effort, you'll do better next time." That's what today's delicate snowflakes would hear. But in the early sixties, if we missed a set or couldn't dig out a spike, we heard comments like, "If you can't make the play, get off the court"; "What are you, stupid?"; "The serve is supposed to go over the net, dumbass; the ball doesn't fit through the little holes in the net." Some may think that those men were too tough on us, but really, they made us better players. The skills and toughness they taught us allowed us to win the volleyball championships in the ten-to-twelve, thirteen-to-fourteen, and fifteen-to-sixteen-year-old age groups in the Woonsocket Park League as well as serve as the foundation for future endeavors. Post–high school, Tom and Kevin became great players on a national level and I was better than average playing on the beach. John and Obie were good, solid volleyball players and found the lessons learned at the Y transferred easily to basketball, their preferred sport long term.

John Zoltek, coach and athletic director for the YMCA, sponsored a major men's volleyball tournament every year at the high school gym. Teams from all over New England, New York, and a few from Canada competed. Coach Zoltek recruited us to be line judges and to run errands during the event. Prior to that year's first serve, he realized that he had left his team's roster in his office back at the Y about a mile away. Per standard tournament rules, all rosters had to be submitted before play could begin. Coach needed someone to go immediately to the Y and retrieve the roster. Tom volunteered to run and get it, but that would take too long. When Zoltek asked Tom if he could drive a car, Tom said, "No, but Doug can." Yes, I drove cars around the gas station parking lot and in and out of the service bays, but I had never driven on the streets. Not to mention, I was only twelve—far from legal age, even in Woonsocket.

Coach Zoltek tossed me the keys to his Ford Falcon convertible and without hesitation, we went to get the roster. Tom called shotgun and jumped into the front seat while Kevin, John, and Obie piled in back seat. This was exciting! An underage driver with four young passengers driving through downtown Woonsocket with the top down and the AM radio playing. As tempted as we were, we made no detours on our mission. We went directly to the Y, retrieved the roster, and delivered it in plenty of time. We then took our places as linesmen. We paid attention to our jobs, but we couldn't stop thinking about how much fun that drive had been. We spent all afternoon thinking of reasons for us to take the car out again. Finally, unwittingly, Coach Z came through. He discovered he also had left some of the awards at the Y. Great guys that we were, we volunteered to again help him out. This trip wasn't as time-critical as our first drive, so we took our places in the Falcon and made a roundabout trip up Park Avenue, down Main Street, and through the North End before going to the Y and picking up the trophies. Talk about virtual reality. We didn't need any devices or video games to see ourselves as quite the cool, mature guys driving through town. We were actually doing it—and loving every minute!

Glad the Horse

Very often when we went to Getchell's, whether it was in the Wikiera-mobile or riding our bikes, we passed a farm that had a great-looking lake. The lake wasn't very big, but it had many access spots where we could cast our lines. Being the fishing experts we fancied ourselves to be, we were positive that this lake had to be loaded with giant, eight-pound bass and we were certain that if we had the opportunity to fish there, we'd end up with our pictures on the front page of the *Woonsocket Call*.

The lake was right in front of a big, white farmhouse— you know, the kind of house tourists riding through the countryside like to see and romanticize about the virtues of pastoral living. We weren't exactly sure the owners would approve of our fishing on their property, so thought it best to not make our presence known. The farmhouse was on one side of the road and the lake was on the other side, about a hundred yards down a hill. Fortunately, in addition to being expert anglers, we also considered ourselves expert problem solvers. Rather than go up to the door and ask for permission, which would be way too easy, we decided to take a sneaky and thrilling route to end up fishing with little chance of being seen. And, if by any chance we were seen, we felt confident our fleet feet would undoubtedly allow our escape with absolutely no chance of being caught.

So, on a made-for-fishing summer day, we pedaled to Castle Hill, the local nine-hole golf course, where we left our bikes. We then followed the railroad tracks that bordered Castle Hill to the backside of the farm. Armed with our fishing gear and avoiding the warm, freshly dropped cow dung, we stealthily worked our way across the pasture on our way to fishing nirvana. Nice guys that we were, we let Tom, as always, carry our worms and lead the way, serving as recon to "sniff out" the plentiful and aromatic land mines. Who knew that cows liked Thai food? In addition to being prolific and smelly defecators, the dairy cows around the water weren't exactly people-friendly; luckily, they did move as we got close to them.

There it was! The lake that held the giant largemouth bass we were positive we could catch. We got closer and the ground got soggier. Then reality hit us hard. Our fishing lake was nothing more than a pond, nothing more than a watering hole for cows. Unfortunately, at the time, we didn't understand the differences between a lake and a pond. Though he knew plenty on the football field, I don't remember Coach Morey teaching our science classes that lakes are deeper and usually have streams or rivers feeding them. A pond is really nothing more than a big puddle with plants growing in it. There weren't any fish at all in this pond, let alone trophy-size bass. Frogs were abundant, but that was about it. Had we been Southerners, maybe we would have stayed around to gig some.

Disappointedly, we headed back across the field, ac-cused each other of being too stupid to recognize a mud hole from a bass lake, and complained that we missed a great day at Getchell's. Of course, none of us would accept the blame for this ill-fated excursion—the same brilliant idea for which we earlier fought over claiming. We started back across the field toward the railroad tracks and Castle Hill. At Castle Hill, we could at least turn the day around and make a dollar or two by pulling some golf balls out of the water hole and selling them in the pro shop.

However, our fortunes quickly turned! Right in front of us was a large gray horse that looked friendly and came right up to us. It was obvious he wanted some attention, so we talked to him and petted him. This was great! What fantastic luck! We thought we had a new pet, and if we were going to have a pet horse, two things needed to be done immediately. We had to name him and ride him. Many names were suggested, but I came up with the creative, yet fitting, name "Glad," because, hey, we were glad we found him. Notice I said we found him. It didn't occur to us that this may be somebody's horse walking around in a fenced pasture—not a stray looking to be adopted. But, for the moment, Glad was ours. The second task, riding him, would prove to be slightly more difficult.

These were the days of TV westerns like *The Lone Ranger*, *Roy Rogers*, and *Bonanza*. We watched a lot of cowboys run and jump on horses; they rode fast and they rode hard. How tough could this be? Indians (yes, that's what they were called back then) rode horses without saddles, so riding Glad should be a piece of cake. Tom volunteered to take the first ride and Glad was very cooperative. Our horse just stood there with John holding the bridle while Kevin and I helped Tom mount the mighty stallion. Tom was seated high and looking proud. As Tom sat there, Glad took a few steps. It would have made a classic portrait. Tom Wikiera astride a big, beautiful, gallant steed. Sadly, there are no pictures of this momentous day. None of us owned a camera; cell phone cameras and the narcissistic addiction to selfies were decades away, and we rarely had our pictures taken anyway. After some coaxing and a few "giddy-ups," Glad walked a few steps. Movement. Tom was riding. We then realized that Glad had a bridle but no reins for Tom to hold on to. I was wearing a long-sleeve shirt, so John, ever generous with other people's things, suggested that I take it off and tie it to the bridle for Tom to use as reins. I complied and Tom was ready to ride.

The ubiquitous "they" say that timing is everything; there can be good timing and there can be bad timing. There are some things we can count on. The sun comes up in the morning and goes down at night. The lovable Red Sox will not compete for the pennant again this year and the bells in the high steeple of the big red church on Blackstone Street will ring every day at noon. Not just ring, but ring so loudly that they could be heard throughout Woonsocket and surrounding areas. We didn't wear watches, so most days the bells served notice to us that we were due home for lunch. Apparently, what we considered as a human reminder also extended to a certain horse recently named Glad, on which Tom happened to be seated. We should have named him Lightning based on the way he took off toward the barn when he heard the bells. Who knew that a horse would understand bells? Apparently, our science classes hadn't gotten to Pavlov either. We watched in amazement as Glad galloped across the field and Tom bounced up and down with absolutely no control, but only for about thirty yards. As John, Kevin, and I chased the getaway steed, Tom Wikiera, a.k.a. Bareback Bucking Bronco Rider, flew up and back. When we reached him we couldn't stop laughing. We asked Tom if he was hurt, then realized that he probably wasn't hurt because, as dumb luck would have it, the fall was broken by a massive pile of freshly dropped cow dung! At least he was wearing a shirt. Our walk back to Castle Hill to get our bikes was a memorable one filled with laughter, jeers, ribbing, and everyone trying to stay upwind of Tom. But again, at least he had a shirt.

One of my part-time jobs was pumping gas at the Flying A gas station across the street from my house. I didn't have many shirts, so losing this one was significant, to say the least. It looked like I would be pumping a lot of gas in order to replace Glad's new reins. No fight broke out during this adventure, but thoughts of punching one or both of the Wikieras surely crossed my mind. And, I often wonder what Glad's owners thought when their horse arrived at the barn wearing my shirt.

The Trip to Fenway Park

Woonsocket had a great recreation system with playgrounds and ball fields spread out around the city in the areas earlier described as villages. Each park employed two college kids as counselors who organized, officiated, and supervised activities ranging from arts and crafts to sports. We had something to do every day of the week, but one of the high points of our summer was the trip to Fenway Park to see our favorite team, the Boston Red Sox. The Woonsocket Rec Department organized a trip to Fenway Park and its famous Green Monster for a midweek day game. For the incredibly low price of one dollar we received the fifty-mile bus ride to Boston, a ticket to the game, a hot dog, and a coke. Because this was a citywide activity, our friends from other parks joined us in a caravan of busses headed to Boston.

During the early sixties, the Red Sox were far from the best team in baseball, but that didn't diminish our love for them. We lived and breathed, laughed and cried with the Boston Red Sox. We knew all the players and most of their stats. We didn't have ESPN and *SportsCenter* to provide updates and highlights, but we did have Robby Rabbit to keep us up-to-date on anything we may have missed.

The Sox were playing the Baltimore Orioles, who were not much better than the Sox. Over the course of the season, which was fairly representative of the early sixties, the Sox won ten out of eighteen games against the Orioles, but the Orioles finished the season one game ahead of the Sox in the league standings. If there was another team that had players we liked, it was the "O's." Everyone admired the players on the Yankees, but none of us liked them as a team because they were, well, as Tom would say, "EVIL!"

Back in the old days of baseball, there was the American League and the National League. There were no divisions or wild-card teams and division play didn't begin until 1969. Until then, each team played 162 games, and at the end of the season, the winner of the American League played the winner of the National League for the World Series title.

Though a tier two team, the Red Sox had two all-stars: starting pitcher Bill Monbouquette (15-13, 3.33 ERA), whom we would see start this game, and first baseman Pete Runnels, who hit .326. Other great players included third baseman Frank Malzone, left fielder Carl "Yaz" Yastrzemski (.296), and a great relief pitcher, Dick Radatz, who finished the season with nine wins, six losses, twenty-four saves, and a 2.24 ERA. Radatz made $7,500 and Yastrzemski $15,000 for the '62 season. Imagine the salaries their stats would have generated in today's game.

The Orioles had some great infielders, such as all-star third baseman Brooks Robinson and Jerry Adair at short-stop. Robin Roberts and Chuck Estrada anchored their pitching staff. The outfield was patrolled by Whitey Herzog, who, in 1982, won the World Series as manager of the St. Louis Cardinals. The Orioles outfield also had Boog Powell, a big power hitter whom Tommy hated for reasons known only to him. I think Boog is still around. Catch a game at Camden Yard and you can enjoy Boog's Barbeque.

This was a day game, and because it was between two not-so-good teams, the crowd was sparse. Our seats were way up in the nosebleed section of the bleachers, but we ran down to the empty field-level box seats. We boldly decided to go where we had never been before—the front row, right next to the visitor's dugout. The ushers chased us away, but we kept going back. After a couple of innings, they finally gave up and watched the game, not us.

The weather was perfect; it couldn't have been a better New England day. There is an incredible sight and feeling when you get to Fenway and walk through the tunnel from the entrance, past the concession area to the field. It's like the first time that you see the theme parks that surround Orlando, Florida—pure magic! What a treat. We had even made a huge banner that exclaimed, "MONBO MEANS PENNANT!" that we proudly paraded after each inning that Bill Monbouquette mowed down the opposition.

The game was scoreless to start the fourth inning. With runners on first and second and two men out, Boog Powell stepped into the batter's box. He was a monster of a man. He had huge arms and legs like tree trunks, muscles everywhere. "Monbo" had his good stuff that day and Boog suffered the same fate that he had experienced his first time at bat: a big "K." Not only did he strike out, but he looked bad, really bad, doing it. No batter feels good about striking out, but being fooled by the pitcher twice in a row and looking like a little leaguer can cause even a professional to get hot.

Tom must have taken a page from the Book of Obie. He felt that this was the perfect opportunity to "get someone's ass." And that someone was Boog Powell. As Boog slowly walked back from the batter's box, Tom started on him. "Atta boy, Boog!" Tom screamed. "I don't blame you for not trying—nobody else is either. Keep it up." Because of his proximity, Boog could hear every word. Tom felt good and Boog felt bad. Tom knew that he was "getting the ass" of a big leaguer.

At the top of the seventh inning, the Sox held a two-run lead. "Monbo" was throwing a shutout against one of the stronger-hitting teams in the majors. We were in the front row watching a classic struggle; the Sox were winning, the bases were loaded, there were two out, and stepping up to the plate was Boog Powell. Wow! Could it have been more dramatic? Tom was on him with every step toward the plate. "Come on, Boog. Keep it up, buddy! You can do it again." With each strike, it seemed that all that could be heard in the entire park was Tom screaming, "Aaaaaaah Haaaaaaa! Eeeeeeee Haaaaaw!" and with the final strike came a howling, "Yaaaahoooo!"

Boog started back to the dugout. With each step, above all the cheers, Tom was screaming even louder, "Atta boy, Boog! I knew you could do it! Thanks for the K! Why should you try when no one else is?"

Apparently, Boog had heard enough. Instead of retiring to the dugout, he veered out of the path, stopped, and stared directly at Tom and yelled, "What the hell are you looking at?" Everyone in the section watched Tom quietly and slowly sit down. The blood had gone from his face and he was completely pale. Pale until John and Obie started on him. Tom's color quickly came back, which signaled Obie to be quiet. But not so John. He kept on ribbing Tom until Tom punched him as hard as he could in the arm. That was the hardest I ever saw Tom hit John, but it worked only temporarily. John struck back and that started a fight. And Boog, who was still looking at Tom, smiled.

Park League Sports

If we weren't fishing, swimming, or off on a bicycle adventure, we could be found at Cold Spring Park. Woonsocket, despite being a poor mill town, had a great Parks and Recreation Department run by department head Bill "Stewie" Renaud. He was a friendly and all-around great guy who was loved by all and was dedicated to providing wonderful summer experiences.

There were six public parks scattered around the city in the areas once known as the villages of Bernon, Cass, Globe, and Social, plus Cold Spring Park in the North End and Dunn Park in Fairmont. They were well maintained and staffed by college students home for summer break. These great places offered kids a place to gather, make friends, and take advantage of supervised activities in arts and crafts, games, and sports. At one time, Bernon, Social, and Globe parks had swimming pools, but they were closed due to the polio scare of the 1950s. Cold Spring Park had a natural spring, hence the name. Cold, fresh water that could quench even the most ravenous thirst flowed out of the spring twenty-four hours a day. Every evening, rain or shine, there would be people lined up to fill their water jugs.

We participated in every sport and activity offered at the park. The highlights of the summer were the last two weeks, when all the parks would compete in games and sports tournaments. Baseball, volleyball, and basketball were the major sports followed by the end of the summer track meet. Sports were organized by age group. Our primary group was the ten-to-twelve age group, but depending on the sport, we also competed in the thirteen-to-fourteen and fifteen-to-sixteen age brackets. Despite being younger than our opponents, we did well and proved that brains, talent, and great coaching cannot be held back. There were no petty jealousies or major conflicts within our group during these times because we were focused on beating everyone else.

We were good little league baseball players and always a contender for the park league baseball championship. Tom and Obie did the pitching along with Duke Dubois and Al Durand. Duke was an exceptional catcher and hitter and Al was a fine all-around athlete. I roamed the outfield, and when a fly ball came my way, there was a 50/50 chance I would catch it. Most outfielders would see a fly ball and yell, "I got it." I would yell, "I'll try." The finals that year pitted us against Cass Park, who had a tremendous pitcher and athlete, Roger Williams. Tom pitched and threw a one-hitter. That one hit by Williams just happened to be a home run. Roger pitched a no-hitter and they beat us 1-0.

In addition to the park league, we belonged to the Woonsocket YMCA, where we played volleyball and basketball. When we were about ten years old, the physical director, Eben "Stocky" Stockbridge, took a select few, the five of us included, and told us that if we wanted to play Saturday-morning basketball, we would have to show up an hour early to learn volleyball. At first, we didn't like it, but Stocky drilled us on how to bump, set, and spike as well as to embrace the game. Stocky's successor, John Zoltek, continued his plan. By the time we were twelve years old, we had no competition on the volleyball court. We knew the game very well, well enough to win the park league championship in all three age brackets. When we started playing volleyball, we didn't realize that Stocky and John Zoltek had an ulterior motive; they were priming us to play for the Y's men's team, a team that, in 1964, would win the national championship. Their plan worked. Tom started playing with the team in 1965 at fifteen years old and Kevin joined in 1975 after college. I never had the opportunity to play for the Y, but while in college, I won the intramural volleyball MVP award and played beach volleyball along the west coast of Florida. Stocky and Zoltek's plan paid off for all of us.

When basketball season arrived, though the tournament was always a challenge, we were a force to be reckoned with. We did very well that year, besting Bernon, Cass, Globe, and Social parks during the regular season. The semifinal match for the championship pitted us against Dunn Park. After winning their semifinals game, the Globe Park team was on the sidelines to cheer us on because they didn't want to again face humiliation at the hands of Dunn Park. During the regular season, we beat Globe by five points and Dunn drubbed them by twenty-two. Winning by twenty-two points is huge when playing eight-minute quarters with a running clock. The Globe team was sure we didn't have a chance to win, but they cheered us on anyway.

Dunn Park was located near the housing projects, which, at the time, were predominately African American. Keep in mind that this was 1962. The civil rights movement was a few years away and the term African American had yet to be coined. To us and most people, these guys were colored, which we didn't use as a pejorative.

Dunn had an impressive team; tall, fast, and intimidating.

They were led by Bob "Needle" Farrow. He was a great all-around athlete, with basketball being his best sport. At age twelve, he was like a man playing against kids. Their second star, Joe Harris, who came from a family of talented athletes, was also tall, quick, and strong. Johnny Abney filled out their top three. He was their ball handler and did a great job setting up the big guys. These three and, let's say, two "less talented" players filled out the lineup that dominated the league. Everyone thought we would get slaughtered just like every other park league team Dunn faced. Everyone, that is, except Tom. Was Tom prescient? I think not. He just didn't believe in losing.

Everyone on our team was about the same size, not much over five-feet. John was our primary outside scorer, followed by Obie and Kevin. Tom and I worked under the boards. We weren't big but we could jump, and Dunn's size didn't scare us. We didn't lose a beat when we substituted with Al Durand and Paul Dubois

There were three reasons we thought we could win. First, we weren't intimidated. No one thought that our skinny white-bread team could beat the big black guys from Dunn with "Needle," their big center dominating the middle. But we would play the game like we played every other game: give 100 percent and whatever happens, happens. Second, we could jump. Tom had a freakish vertical leap and could almost touch the rim. John, Al, and I weren't far behind. Third, we were quick, we hustled, and we weren't afraid to dive for loose balls on the outside concrete court. There wasn't a lot of room along the sidelines. if you went too far out of bounds you were on your way down a hill. Not exactly a great landing pad when we dived for balls, but that didn't stop us. The backboards were metal, and the nets were chain, not nylon. Rather than hearing *swoosh* on a score, we heard *clang*—and loved it!

We also had something that Dunn didn't have—a coach, fourteen-year-old Willie Barr. Willie was a fantastic player who, with Bob Farrow, would later win the thirteen-to-fourteen and fifteen-to-sixteen championships. But Willie wasn't just a player, he was a student of the game. He drilled us the same way his high school coach, Vinnie Dwyer, drilled him. Willie would tell us, "When playing against bigger, faster athletes, you have to move when the ball moves, not follow it with your eyes and then react." Willie was also familiar with every player on the Dunn team and knew their strengths and their weaknesses. On defense, we played man-to-man. He told us whom to guard and how to do it. Tom stuck to Needle and I to Joe like glue. Willie had us play a slow and deliberate offense that slowed down Dunn's fast and powerful game plan. On offense, we ran plays that got John, Obie, and Kevin open and Tom and I fed them the ball. Willie's slow-down offense helped us keep the score close, which would give us a chance to eke out a win.

Dunn also had a solid game plan. They knew that Tom and I had little chance of scoring on Needle and Joe, so all that they had to do was play tenacious defense against John, Obie, and Kevin. John Abney was a good defensive player, but Dunn's other two players were not.

It was a heck of a basketball game. The first three periods ended in scores of 3 to 3, 6 to 6, and 9 to 9. Willie's game plan worked as we had hoped. In the last period, John and Obie heated up and we put them away 16-12.

We were elated, as was the team from Globe Park. They thought they had a chance to beat us and win the championship with Dunn out of the way. The championship game was anticlimactic. Globe's happiness soon turned to utter humiliation, as by the end of the first period, they were hopelessly behind and destroyed both physically and mentally. We were riding high after our big win and we weren't going to let up. John, Obie, and Kevin were far too fast and quick for the Globe team to keep up with while Tom and I completely dominated both the offensive and defensive boards. It ended as a blowout!

We were fortunate that Woonsocket had such a great park league that gave us opportunities in multiple sports. There were no league fees or expensive equipment requirements. Except for baseball gloves, everything was provided.

We finished the park league tournament season with a second in baseball, three age-group volleyball titles, and a basketball championship. We were proud, and there were no fights.

Par for the Course

As young boys growing up in the early sixties, no one suggested we specialize in only one sport. There were no limits to the sports that we played or attempted to play. And dreams of success accompanied our efforts. Baseball, football, and basketball were our primary sports with volleyball moving up the ladder, but we were willing to try anything that involved a ball and competition.

About one half mile from our homes, in the North End of Woonsocket and sharing the border with Blackstone, Massachusetts, was Castle Hill Country Club. It was a nine-hole course, short but relatively difficult. Unlike many of the courses I've played in Florida, this one didn't have houses and condos lining the fairways. As with most golf courses in New England, it was probably once a cow pasture that was converted to a golf course. There were a lot of hills and valleys, ledge rock showing in many places; a lot of trees, bushes, and briars; and two water holes. During the winter months, this was a great venue for sledding and ice-skating. There was a huge swampy section in the middle of the fairway on the fifth hole. The first tee was the highest point on the course with a great view of holes 1, 4, and 5. Past the fairways were railroad tracks, the same tracks we followed into Blackstone and the pasture where we met Glad the horse. The tee boxes were small platforms made up of compressed cardboard set into six-by-four-foot metal frames. It was a very inexpensive, working man's golf course. To us, it was the Woonsocket equivalent to Augusta National.

The owners of the course were two nice brothers who had children our age, and with whom we went to school. We weren't regular golfers, but we played often enough to be friendly with the owners. Greens fees were two dollars, but if we got there early on a Monday or Tuesday morning, we could work off the fee by picking up trash and raking the sand traps. The owners also allowed us to borrow clubs.

One day, we decided that the four of us were going to have a golf match. Our competition wouldn't be like the legendary one featured in Mark Frost's book *The Match: The Day the Game of Golf Changed Forever*, a 1956 four-ball event that pitted two of the greatest professional golfers of the era, Byron Nelson and Ben Hogan, against top amateurs Harvie Ward and Ken Venturi. Our match was neither as skilled nor as civilized. We made arrangements with the owners, got up early, went to the course, completed the greens fee requirements, and were ready for our big event. After a few minutes of intense arguments, we all agreed that the fairest way that we could do this was to have two teams, and whichever player from a team had the better score, that team would get a point for the hole. We assumed, of course, that because there were nine holes there would have to be a winning team. Normally, the teams would be predetermined; John and Kevin on one team, Tom and I on the other. But golf was a different sport. John and Kevin, though they rarely played, were rather good golfers. They both had fluid swings and the ability to turn their hips in sync with their upper bodies, which resulted in decent yardage. They were also fairly consistent. My game was steady, but not as precise or steady as John's and Kevin's.

Tom's game was easy to describe; it was bad on his best days. From the moment he put a driver in his hands, nothing good was going to happen. He swung the driver with an inside-out baseball swing, and while some golfers have a slice, his was more of a boomerang, ball curving farther to the right with each try. The only time he could hit a fairway was when he aimed far to the left and sliced the ball back to the right. This technique wasn't foolproof. Occasionally he would hit the dreaded straight ball and end up in the woods, on the railroad tracks, or on Edmund Street. He did manage to hit fairway irons slightly straight, and probably should have used them off the tee, but he was too stubborn to try. With the putter, he possessed the touch of a gorilla. He was truly a "hacker." As the old joke went, "If you looked up the word *hacker* in the dictionary, you'd see his picture." The truth of the matter was that the chances of any of us making it through any hole without at least one extremely bad shot were slim.

It was relatively easy to determine the teams. Kevin and John had to be split up and John and Tom could not be on the same team. It was agreed that Kevin and Tom would play against John and me, and the losers would buy sodas after the match. The sad truth about these pairings, which on paper looked like John and I had the advantage, was that we were actually at a disadvantage. Golf is a game of honor. One must have self-control and the dignity to play the game by the rules to which I always tried to adhere. All three of my buddies shared my philosophy, but when playing golf, they just happened to explain their philosophies a little differently. John believed that golf should be played using "a preferred lie." In his mind, that meant he preferred to lie—lie about where he was, how he got there, and how many strokes it took him to get there. Kevin, who excelled in math, believed that "if you're keeping score and you can't win, there is something wrong with you!" Tom, who was never subtle, lived by "win if you can, lose if you must, but always cheat!" In reality, the match was two against one.

We began with the course almost entirely to ourselves. John teed off first and hit the ball down the hill to the left behind a tree. I hit a good ball, straight but not as far as John's. Kevin pushed his shot off to the right and Tom duffed his shot off the tee, his straightest tee shot of the day, and with the fortunate downhill roll was about forty yards past the tee. It was his first shot of many that day. I beat the odds on that hole, made four decent shots in a row, made my only par of the day, and we were up 1-0.

The second hole ran parallel to the first except that it was uphill and there was a rugged forested, briar-filled rocky area to the right. John and I imploded, Tom sliced into the woods, and Kevin played less poorly than the rest of us to take the hole.

The third hole ran parallel to one and two and was narrow. Most golfers have holes on which they typically play well and confidently attack. The third hole belonged to John. Tom sliced into the woods again and lost another ball. The good news was that he and Kevin found four balls and came out smiling despite losing the hole.

Number four was an intimidating par-three water hole. There were trees, rocks, and briars to the left, a monster tree on the right, and a large, shallow waterhole right in front of the green. John buried his drive into the hilly rock formation to the left, Kevin and I found the water, and Tom sliced his shot far into the fifth fairway. The one thing that we didn't want to do when playing golf was to lose balls, so Kevin and I went into the water, John climbed the hill, and Tom went for a hike. There is something about young boys and water that usually leads to horseplay. I found two balls and Kevin found a frog, which he decided to throw, and hit me squarely in the back. I retaliated quickly with what I had at hand—mud! It splattered over his entire upper body. Not to be left out, and holding the high ground, John launched a large rock into the water, which splashed both of us. The second rock that John threw drove us out of the water and reminded us to get back to the game. As the three of us met just off the green to discuss how we were going to handle our penalty shots and where we were going to place our balls, Tom unleashed his second shot from a long way off. It was an incredible shot, bouncing twice, hitting the flagpole squarely, and dropping two inches from the hole. Tom parred the hole! The three of us watched in awe and immediately tried to figure out how he had cheated or what he had done to make such a shot. Maybe he had moved his ball closer to the green. But it didn't matter how he did it; the proof was right in front of us and we saw it with our own eyes. He had made the shot of the day. For us to walk back to the tee and re-tee shooting three didn't make sense, so we ceded the hole, and after four holes we were all tied up.

The next four holes were uneventful. We had our share of arguments over balls that were kicked forward or thrown backward, strokes that weren't counted, and the ball that I hit into the woods that John "found" five yards into the fairway. When it was over, Kevin had taken two holes and John had taken the other two, so we were tied at four apiece.

The walk from the eighth green to the ninth tee was a

somber one. There was no trash talk or heckling. It's a good thing that Obie wasn't with us. John and Kevin were quiet, and it was obvious to me that the two thinkers—or as Tom called them, the two stinkers—were plotting ways to steal a win in our little tournament. Each of them had quite an imagination. Here we were all tied up at the final hole, and we all knew what was at stake—and it wasn't the sodas; it was bragging rights and being able to rub the win in the faces of the losers. The ninth hole was a par four, about 320 yards long. The green could not be seen from the tee, as the ground rose in between. Along the left were thick bushes and briars. The right side dropped quickly for a long way.

Kevin had the honors and his drive was straight as an arrow, but we lost sight of it as it cleared the rise. Tom, true to form, sliced his tee shot way down the hill. John's shot, with a slight fade, was similar to Kevin's, and though we lost sight of it, we knew that it was close to Kevin's. I hooked my ball into the bushes, and while John and I searched for my ball, Kevin helped Tom search for his. John gave up looking for mine and headed quickly to his ball. They say that timing is everything. Just as John was reaching Kevin's ball, which was farther away from the green than his, Kevin's and Tom's heads were visible over the hill. That meant that John could see them, and they could see John from the shoulders up. The farther they walked up the hill, the more they could see of each other. It was impossible for John to tamper with Kevin's ball, because as soon as he bent down, there would have been an uproar and, of course, the mandatory fight. As Kevin and Tom got closer, Kevin asked John where his ball was and John said, "I don't know. I've been trying to find it for you; my ball is up there ahead. Your ball must have hit a rock and bounced into the woods. You're going to have to take a stroke and drop the ball somewhere near my ball." He pointed up ahead toward his ball.

As Tom and Kevin continued the search for the ball, John didn't move from the spot except for turning in circles in a vain attempt to look for Kevin's ball. It was obvious to me that John was standing on Kevin's ball so that he couldn't find it and would be penalized a stroke for a lost ball. I believe in playing fair, but I also like to win and chose not to say anything about my teammate. No one knew John's evil ways better than Tom, and when he looked up and saw John standing in the exact spot that he had been standing, he yelled to Kevin, "Take a look under John's foot!"

John tried to explain that he must have stepped on the ball by mistake, thinking it was a rock, but no one was buying it. I'd like to say that a fight broke out, but when lightweights like Kevin and John squared off, the conflict was little more than pushing, name-calling, and slaps at each other. Both Tom and I were disappointed. Just then a foursome of real golfers was reaching the green on the eighth hole, and we knew it was time to finish our match. John and Kevin finished the hole with the same score and our tournament ended in a draw. Though nobody won, the lies, exaggerations, and accusations continued for many years.

Shooting the Rapids

Whitewater rafting is a popular daredevil activity for thrill seekers on challenging rivers across the country. Montana has the Yellowstone River, in Colorado, you can ride the Arkansas River, and down in Georgia, the Toccoa River is the place to go.

Unfortunately, we didn't have any rapids, challenging or otherwise, to conquer in Woonsocket. The Blackstone River was slow and lazy. In the summer, we used old car-tire inner tubes to float downstream from Getchell's to Harris Pond, and eventually to Social Ocean, which afforded lots of fun but no real challenge, speed, or danger.

Getchell's, a favorite spot of ours, sets the scene of yet another reckless but fun endeavor. This particular tale doesn't include a runaway horse, fishing, or hooks to the head. In a particularly cold, icy February, Getchell's dam broke. We had no idea why. Probably—like a great deal of New England's infrastructure and denizens—it was just old and past its useful life. The water where we fished for bass and trout was literally on its way out. The landing area for the Tarzan swing where we once landed in cool, clear water was fast becoming a beach of dirt and rocks. The water was rushing downstream and Getchell's Lake would soon be gone.

However, the broken dam did create a great chance for adventure. John had the brilliant idea that he and I should shoot the rapids before the lake was completely empty. So what if it was February and the water was freezing? We didn't know what hypothermia was, and even if we did, it wouldn't have stopped us. It also didn't matter that we had no whitewater experience, much less skills. No way could we pass up this once-in-a-lifetime opportunity.

To ride the rapids, one obviously needs a raft or a canoe. We had no such watercraft. So, we started making phone calls to our friends asking if they had or knew anyone who had a rubber raft or canoe. We struck out. But did that deter us? Of course not. We started going through backyards around the North End, looking through garage windows, assuming we could always "borrow" someone's canoe. We struck out there too.

Fortunately, we ran into Larry Brown and described our plight. Getchell's was emptying fast and we needed to take advantage of the rapids. After a few minutes, Larry came up with a solution. There was an old airplane engine cover in his backyard. Larry's father was some sort of collector and planned on using the cover for who knows what. Larry said we could borrow it as long as we swore to bring it back. The engine cover was just a metal shell about eight-feet-long, tapered at each end, and maybe about ten-inches-deep with a rounded bottom. Even with our lack of useful knowledge from our science teacher, Coach Morey, we knew that a round bottom wouldn't provide very much stability. Not exactly a seaworthy vessel, but better than nothing. The engine cover didn't come with paddles, so we settled for two brooms found in a neighbor's garage and started planning our whitewater adventure.

Getchell's dam was about fifty yards from the road; the stream flowed under a bridge, then curved to the left and meandered downstream. Along the way it passed Harris Pond (another of our fishing holes) and Social Ocean, then ended at the Blackstone River.

Neither of us knew that whitewater streams and rivers were rated by a class system, with Class I being the easiest and safest and Class VI being the wildest and hardest to maneuver. Though we didn't know then that a rating system existed, in retrospect, we feel certain that Getchell's had to be a solid V, which according to the American Whitewater Association's International Scale of River Difficulty are "extremely difficult, long, with very violent rapids and highly congested routes which should be scouted from shore. Should a rescue be needed, conditions are difficult, and there is a significant hazard to life in the event of a mishap."

Feeling confident about our skills and destination, we didn't feel much need to really map our voyage. There was no reason to scout from shore because we had floated down this stream many, many times (albeit under different conditions), so we felt quite sure that we knew every rock and turn. No rescue was anticipated, so no plan needed for that. And, being ignorant, naïve, and short on funds, we surely didn't have life vests, wet suits, or proper clothes. What we did have was a sense of adventure and the guts to try just about anything.

Actually, I guess we did work out what we thought was a logical, foolproof plan. Larry Brown would give us, our watercraft, and brooms a ride to Getchell's. He would drop us off, watch us make the first turn, then drive to Harris Pond to pick us up. Perfect! During the winter months, it was dark by at 5:00 p.m. in Woonsocket, so we would start at about 3:00, which would give us plenty of time to make our ride and get home for dinner. We planned this as a weekday adventure because we feared Getchell's would be empty by the weekend. John and I were sure that we could easily raft from Getchell's to

Harris Pond. It was only about a mile or so, and with the speed of the flowing water, we could easily make the trip before dark. How hard could it possibly be?

We met at Larry's house and phase one was underway. We loaded our engine cover and brooms in the back of his father's station wagon. Then it was off to Getchell's. Phase two, we found a relatively smooth spot to launch. Larry held the shell steady as John got in front and I settled in behind him. Larry gave us a shove and we started downstream. Nothing to it! Had we been more observant or scouted our route, we would have noticed that the stream was about four times wider than before the dam broke. It was also a lot deeper, and definitely moving a lot faster. The round bottom on the engine cover didn't allow us to move very much, so we carefully used our brooms to paddle out to the fast-moving water in the middle. Phase three had us moving downstream and around the corner. Larry waited until he saw us turn the corner, and he then headed for our Harris Pond rendezvous. Traveling down the stream in the rushing waters was fantastic. We were moving much faster than expected and we were loving every minute—until we went sideways and hit a tree. John went up the tree like a squirrel and didn't even get wet. I was hanging on to the tree with both hands while attempting to hold the engine cover with my feet so we wouldn't lose it. Damn, that water was cold. I now had a better appreciation of how Tom felt when he went into the Blackstone River when we were sliding down the hill near Cold Spring Park.

It didn't take long for me to abandon ship and climb the tree. John and I were now sitting in a tree surrounded by rushing water. We discussed our options. One, sit in the tree for a few months until the water receded and we could walk to shore; or two, jump in the water and attempt to fight the current and make our way to shore.

Option two it was. We jumped into the rushing, chest-high, frigid water and fought our way to dry land. It wasn't easy. We couldn't take a straight path to shore because the ever-increasing width of the stream and the speed of the current was pushing us downstream. Trees, brush, and weeds ambushing us from all directions didn't ease our path either. We pushed on and when we reached land, we were exhausted, freezing, and about a mile from Harris Pond where Larry was supposed to pick us up.

With adrenaline flowing and teeth chattering, John and I started running to Harris Pond. We were 100 percent soaked to the skin and had to run just to generate some heat. It took us about fifteen or twenty minutes to get to our meeting point with Larry, but as they say in Woonsocket, "There he was, gone." He didn't know we sank; he assumed we passed the pickup point, so he went home. That left us another two miles or more of a miserable, foot-sloshing, shivering, swearing-at-Larry hike toward some place of refuge from the elements and parental knowledge. We headed for—where else?—the YMCA, where we could get a hot shower and dry our clothes in the sauna. It was a miserable trip. We were cold, wet, exhausted—but we didn't care. We did it! We shot the rapids. Surely, hopefully, forever unknown to Larry Brown's father, we made history as the only people to shoot the rapids on Getchell's stream. As they say in Woonsocket, "La vie est good."

The End

The sixties were a great time for us. Sports, fishing, bike riding, fruit raids, and other adventures created a lifetime of fantastic memories. Memories that we love to share with anyone who will listen. Thank you, dear readers, for allowing us to share them with you. All our years together were wonderful, but the early sixties stand out as the best.

As we moved through junior high and high school, our time together became less frequent. Puberty kicked in, we discovered girls, and they became quite interesting. We played in different leagues and weren't always teammates on the same football or basketball teams anymore, and sometimes we were competitors.

Based on the stories you've read, you may find it hard to believe, but we did mature and lead successful lives. Tom, John, Kevin, and I went to universities and graduated without the massive student loans of today's students. As kids, we were not stupid, we just did some questionable things. Mr. Wikiera once said to John, "Be smart." John laughed and said it was the dumbest thing he ever heard. Of course, he was smart and would continue to be. As stories have told, in John's mind, he was the smartest guy in the world.

After graduating from the University of Rhode Island, where he spent some time on the football team as a linebacker, Tom made a career in the finance and insurance industries. His athletic life continued primarily with volleyball. He was a great volleyball player, one of the best in

New England. With incredible jumping ability, he could spike a ball straight down and have it rebound to the gym ceiling. Not bad for a guy who was only five-foot-nine. He played on many championship teams, winning tournaments all over the Northeast and Canada. Following his playing days, Tom used his expertise and knowledge to coach and develop many high school and college volleyball championship teams and players. He is, to date, of those who coached more than one season, the winningest coach percentagewise in the history of both Woonsocket High School and Rhode Island College. Mixed in with volleyball, Tom married and had two children.

John also graduated from the University of Rhode Island, and, like Tom, spent some time on the football team as a backup quarterback and punt returner. He followed his BA with an MA in psychology. He never really established a career, but rather fancied himself a local expert on everything. Remember, he was smart. John spent much of his free time fishing and pontificating. Name a topic and he was an expert willing to share his insights with anyone who would listen, or buy him a beer and pretend to listen.

Kevin graduated from the University of Tampa and later from Suffolk Law School. He followed in the footsteps of his brother and father and became a cop with the Woonsocket Police Department. After a few years as a patrolman, he left the police force to practice law. He worked as a prosecutor, first in Rhode Island and later in Hawaii. He returned to Rhode Island in the mid-1990s and started a private practice, which was short-lived. Scholastically, Kevin was one of the brightest people I ever knew, and I'm sure he would have kicked butt on *Jeopardy*. In college, he took a five-hour calculus class because for him, it was an easy five-hour A. But somehow, the commonsense boat left the dock without him. And like John, career-wise, nothing really stuck.

Obie didn't attend college. He remained in Woonsocket and made a career with the Public Works Department. He was a better-than-average baseball player and played on the local adult league teams. Like millions of other people from the Northeast, he retired and is now living in Florida.

I graduated from the University of Tampa with a degree in physical education and taught physical education for nine years. After five years of teaching, I went back to school, studied computer science, and changed careers from teaching to the information technology field. My primary sports were fast-pitch softball (I pitched my only no-hitter when I was fifty) and karate/kickboxing, competing in two professional kickboxing matches (1 and 1 record). I married but had no children.

As I mentioned at the beginning, the last time all five of us were together was in the mid-1990s at a sports bar in Woonsocket called Box Seats. Time and distance didn't diminish our friendships; we picked up right where we left off. Laughing, busting chops, and just enjoying each other's company. We drank some beers and told old stories, and, like just about every chapter in this book, Tom and John argued about dates, times, and details of every story, game, event, or whatever. Well, you get it; they disagreed on everything, and when they did find some common ground, Obie would interject and get the battle going again.

We had a few more beers and told more stories before we called it a night. We went through the usual "we'll stay in touch and meet again soon" comments. The evening was easy and fun, but the five of us would never get together again. Tom is retired in Massachusetts, Obie in Florida, and I in Georgia. Unfortunately, Kevin and John left this planet for greener pastures. We miss them, but on the other hand, if they were involved in this writing, the book would have been one thousand pages of crap and still not finished.

I hope you enjoyed our stories and adventures. Tom and I had a great time writing this book and even more fun regaling our wives with our exploits. Truth be told, my wife, Donna, and Tom's wife, Mary Ann, have heard our stories so often, they could have written the book.

Time rapidly passes us. Reach out to your old friends and see how they are doing. You'll be glad you did.

Acknowledgments

DOUG BROOKS

I would like to dedicate this book to the friends, teammates, opponents, and coaches I had the pleasure of knowing. Their influence and inspiration through athletics taught me many lessons that guided me through life. I would like to specifically thank Tom, John, Kevin, and Jim "Obie" for their many years of friendship and memories. Also, thank you to Paul "Duke" Dubois, Al Durand, Bob Farrow, Carl Kociuba, and Willie Barr.

I would like to thank my dad, who patiently sat through many of my games and cheered for me in good weather and bad.

It has been a privilege to have Tom Wikiera as a lifelong friend and wonderful writing partner on this project.

I would also like to thank my good friends, Jim Thomas and Bill Kinsella, for their support and encouragement.

Bruce Hoffman's advice and encouragement were instrumental in getting me on track and moving this book forward.

Thank you to Dr. Nicholas Shaheen, Tom's son-in-law, and my brother in-law, Henry Dewhurst, who took the time and the effort to edit some of the pictures in this book.

Finally, I would like to thank my wife, Donna, for her support, editing skills, and patience.

TOM WIKIERA

I would like to thank the following friends and influences in my life.

Eben Stockbridge, the physical director at the Woonsocket YMCA, brought us all together on basketball teams and forced us to play volleyball, a game we learned to love.

John Zoltek succeeded Eben Stockbridge as the physical director at the YMCA. As the captain and coach of the men's volleyball team, he helped to make me the player and coach that I became and deserves a lot of credit for the success that I achieved. He was a dear friend until he passed away in 2016.

Harris Mathieu Jr. spent a lot of time working with me on the volleyball court and at the beach. He helped me develop and hone my volleyball skills and is still a close friend.

Greg Green was the sports editor of the *Woonsocket Call* and he could be seen at every sporting event, every night that took place in the city. He knew each of us and treated us well in the paper.

Leo Gartsu, a good friend from the YMCA who became my assistant coach at Rhode Island College, was a critical factor in the huge success that we experienced there. He was my mentor, confidant, psychiatrist, best friend, and the best man at my wedding.

My parents, who were my greatest cheerleaders and influence in my life.

I would also like to thank Doug, my best friend growing up, for giving me the opportunity to make contributions to his longtime dream.

About the Authors

Doug Brooks graduated from Woonsocket High School and the University of Tampa. Athletics continued to be a major part of his life as he competed in volleyball, karate/ kickboxing, and fast-pitch softball. He now plays golf, sporting a single-digit handicap. He retired from the high-tech industry in 2013 and lives in Duluth, Georgia.

Tom Wikiera was recruited onto the Woonsocket YMCA Men's Volleyball Team, a nationally ranked squad that won many national tournaments along the East Coast and Canada. He became the most successful volleyball coach at Woonsocket High School and Rhode Island College and was inducted into the Athletic Hall of Fame in each school. Prior to retiring, he worked in the financial sector. His wife of thirty-six years, Mary Ann, and he have two children and reside in Bellingham, Massachusetts.

This is Doug and Tom's first attempt at writing anything longer than a letter to the editor.